VISUAL VOCA 333 Intermediate

TPR 이론의 창시자 | Dr.James J. Asher

휴스턴 대학과 뉴멕시코 대학에서 텔레비전 저널리즘과 심리학으로 박사 학위를 받았다. 그 후, 워싱턴 대학과 스탠포드 대학에서 언어학, 교육심리학의 연구 생활을 계속하였다. 그는 외국어 과목에서 성적이 매우 우수하였음에도 불구하고 말하는 데에 어려움을 겪은 것을 계기로 외국어 교습법에 관심을 갖고 연구를 하여 오른쪽 뇌를 이용한 기억 방식 이론을 창안하였다. 그의 교육이론은 현재 전세계 국가에 널리 활용되며 언어 교육의 가장 효과적인 교습법으로 검증되었다.

기획 | 영춘선생

MBC 생방송 화제집중, SBS 출발 모닝와이드, KBS 시사투나잇에 소개된 UCC 스타 영어 강사 타이거 마스크를 쓰고 영어를 강의하는 영춘선생의 모토는 '영어 공부는 무조건 재미있어야 한다' 로 그의 영어 강의 동영상은 항상 유행어와 웃음이 가득하다. 영춘닷컴(www.youngchoon.com)의 대표로 일하면서 영어 왕초보들이 겪는 고민들을 직접 만나서 듣고 기획한 이 책은 영어 왕초보들에게 반드시 도움이 될 것이다.

영어1팀

Dian Escurel, Ella Banta, Jocelyn Cabigon, Ma. Lourdes Madrona,
Jacquline Morados, Miguel Angelo Villanueva, Carmela Arillo, April Diana Say-ao
다년간 영어를 처음 배우는 한국 사람들만을 대상으로 온라인 영어 강의를 진행해 오고 있으며 오랜 강의를 바탕으로 한국인들에게 적합한 영어 문장을 선택하였다.

영어2팀

Kayla Wilson and Devin Wilson
미국, 캐나다, 영국에 거주하다 지금은 한국에서 영어를 가르치고 있으며 이 책은 실제 원어민들이 많이 쓰는 문장으로 구성하였다.

번역 | 정대단

서울대학교 법과대학 졸업 후 프리랜서 번역사로 활동 중.

일러스트 | 김민재 www.kitschkim.com **손지연** www.sonspree.com **조현아** www.johyuna.com

ENGLISH ICE BREAK
VISUAL VOCA 333 INTERMEDIATE

1판 1쇄 발행 2009년 6월 22일 **1판 3쇄 발행** 2009년 6월 29일
펴낸이 정중모 **펴낸곳** Watermelon English Company **기획** 영춘선생 **책임편집** 김계향
디자인 김해연 이아림 **제작** 송정훈 윤준수 **영업** 남기성 김정호 김경훈 박치우
관리 김명희 박금란 김은경 **등록** 2003년 9월 3일(제300-2003-162호)
주소 서울시 마포구 동교동 203-52 **전화** 02-3144-3700 **팩스** 02-3144-0775
홈페이지 www.engicebreak.com **이메일** editor@yolimwon.com

* 책값은 뒤표지에 있습니다.
ISBN 978-89-7063-626-9 14740
ISBN 978-89-7063-624-5 14740 (세트)

VISUAL VOCA 333

★ Don't Study!

★ Don't Repeat!

★ Just Imagine & Listen

Watermelon

★ 이 책을 위한 친절한 영춘선생의 부가 설명

1. boyfriend는 boy와 friend가 합쳐진 단어입니다
333단어 안에 boyfriend는 없고 boy와 friend라는 단어가 있기 때문에
Boyfriend는 한 단어로 취급하였습니다. (girlfriend 또한 한 단어로 하였습니다.)
-

2. 영어를 처음 배우는 초보자들을 위하여 단축형을 사용하지 않았습니다
물론 영어에서 단축형을 사용할 때 말의 의미가 달라지겠지만
지금 꼭 알아야 하는 것은 아닙니다. ex) don't, doesn't, let's, isn't 등
-

3. 이 책은 영어를 처음 배우는 초보자를 위해 한글 번역 시 최대한 직역을 하였습니다
직역을 원칙으로 했으나 의미 전달이 되지 않을 때에는 일부 의역을 하였습니다.

4. 한 단어가 문장 내에서 다양하게 쓰이는 것을 보여 주려고 여러 뜻으로 번역하였습니다
예를 들면, You의 경우도 당신, 너 등의 여러 가지 표현을 사용한 이유 또한
다양한 표현으로 사용되는 예를 보여주려는 것입니다.

5. 단어의 그림은 일반적으로 많이 쓰이는 뜻으로 그렸습니다
-

6. 그림을 보고 1초 만에 이해가 안 간다고 화내시면 안됩니다
이 책을 미리 학습하신 분들께서 그림을 보며 고민했던 영어 문장이 더욱 오래 기억에 남는다고
하였습니다. 그래서 중요하다고 생각되는 문장은 의도적으로 한번 더 생각하는 그림으로 그렸습니다.
영어는 영어 자체로 이해하는 것이 가장 빨리 영어를 습득할 수 있는 방법입니다.
번역을 붙인 이유는 사전을 찾아야 하는 번거로움을 덜기 위해서지 번역을 보고 한글로 이해를 하라는
것이 절대 아닙니다. 완벽한 번역을 원하시는 분은 번역 관련 책을 보고 직접 번역을 해 보면 학습
효과가 더욱 상승됩니다. 완벽한 번역이 끝나신 분은 영춘선생께 연락 부탁드립니다.
(영춘선생과의 '무료 일일 데이트 초대장'을 제공해 드리겠습니다.)

Preface

1500단어도 아니고 500단어도 아닌 333단어가 부담이 되나요?

이 책의 그림을 통해 333개의 단어를 자연스럽게 익힐 수 있습니다. 자연스럽게 익힌 단어를 바로 1800여 개의 문장으로 만할 수 있게 구성되었습니다.

333단어만 알면 2단어로 구성되어 있는 문장에서 12단어로 구성된 문장까지 당신의 입으로 1800문장을 말할 수 있습니다

막연히 영어가 어렵다고 생각하는 분들을 위해 만들어신 책으로 가만히 따라가다 보면 어느새 영어와 친해져 있는 여러분의 모습을 발견하게 됩니다.

지겨운 연습장과 펜은 치워버리고 눈으로만 보세요

이 책은 전체가 그림으로 표현된 영어 책입니다. 그림이 주는 효과는 크게 두 가지인데, 하나는 보는 즉시 내용을 알게 해 준다는 것과 또 하나는 우뇌를 자극해 기억하기 쉽게 해 주는 것입니다.

망각 곡선에 근거한 자연스런 반복

이 책에 나와있는 333개의 단어들은 불규칙적으로 여러 번 반복됩니다. 보통 7번 정도의 우연한 만남이 있어야 대상을 확실히 기억할 수 있다고 하는데 자연스런 반복을 통해 영어의 기본을 여러 분 몸에 확실히 익힐 수 있게 도와 줄 것입니다.

How to use this book

이 책 하나로 영어 읽기, 말하기 그리고 듣기를 동시에

① [영어 읽기] 책에 있는 그림을 보면서 단어와 문장을 눈으로 읽습니다

그림을 보며 단어와 문장을 익힙니다.
그림으로 한눈에 문장을 이해할 수 있게
도와줍니다.

---

② [영어 듣기] Visual Voca 333 Mp3를 청취합니다

MP3를 들으면서 원어민의 정확한 발음을 익히고
미리 보았던 그림을 상상하면서 들어 보세요.
그림으로 기억된 문장과 Mp3파일이 함께
머릿속에 기억 되면 본인이 영어로
말을 해야 할 때 어렵지 않게
문장을 떠올릴 수 있습니다.

---

③ [말하기] Review 부분을 소리 내어 읽는다

각 Chapter 들이 끝난 후 Review 페이지에는 영어 문장과 그림이
나와있습니다. Review 부분을 소리 내어 읽으면서 영어를 익힙니다.
박지성 선수의 축구 경기를 아무리 많이 봐도 박지성 선수의 축구
실력이 되지 않는 것은 직접 운동장에서 공을 차지 않기 때문입니다.
영어를 아무리 많이 들어도 본인이 직접
소리 내어 말하지 않는다면
영어는 늘지 않습니다.

Talk, talk and talk about this book

"공부하는 책이라기보다는 만화책 같은 책"

이런 종류의 책이 최근에 많이 나와서 또 그런 책이 나왔구나 라고 생각했는데 333단어의 한정적인 수로 1800문장을 만든 다는 게 끌려서 읽어 봤는데 술술 넘어 가다 보니 어느 덧 12단어로 된 문장까지 구사가 가능하더군요. 놀랍습니다.

배민성, 32세, 영국 유학 준비중

"문법에는 자신이 있지만 항상 영어 말하기가 문제였습니다"

중고등학교 때 배웠던 문법은 기억이 나지만 영어 말하기가 항상 문제였습니다. 이 책을 보고 나서 이렇게 영어로 말하는 게 쉬운지 몰랐습니다. 좋은 책을 만들어 주신 영춘선생님께 감사드립니다.

문민호, 31세, 대학원생

영어 읽기, 말하기, 듣기까지 동시에 다 할 수 있는 책이네요

김나영, 29, 패션디자이너

그림으로 단어와 문장을 기억하니까 훨씬 쉽게 외우고 더 오래 기억되는 것 같아요!

김현진, 29세, 직장인

단어가 계속 반복되어서 외우기 싫어도 그냥 외워져요

김영기, 27세, 대학원생

눈으로만 공부할 수 있다는 게 이런 거군요. 그리고 책이 너무 예뻐서 계속 보게 돼요

장세희, 31세, 대학원생

내 아들이 기획한 책이라서가 아니라 정말 뒤늦은 나이에 영어 공부를 다시 시작할 수 있게 만들어 준 책이에요

노혜정, 58세, 어린이집 교사

진짜 333단어로 1800문장을 말할 수 있어요

신요한, 32세, 사회복지사

| **영어 왕초보**를 위해 드리는 **영춘선생**의 **영어 공부 설명서** |

한국에서 나오는 많은 영어 관련 서적이나 학습법을 보면 정말 이런 학습 방법들이 '정말 영어 왕초보에게 도움이 되나?' 라는 생각이 듭니다.
대부분 쉽게 배우는 영어 학습법이라고는 하지만 대부분의 한국인들에게 해당하는 영어 왕초보들은 여전히 영어공부가 어렵습니다.

아래는 많은 영어 전문가 분들께서 추천하시는 국내에서 익히는 영어 학습법입니다.

　　　길가는 원어민을 헌팅하세요
____ 자! 헌팅을 했다 치자 말이 안 통하는데 뭘 어떻게 하라는지. 입장은 바꿔서, 길가는 외국인이 한국어를 배우려고 당신을 헌팅했다고 치자 길가던 당신이 그 외국인이 정말 화려한 외모가 아닌 이상에 당신이 한국어를 가르쳐 줄까

　　　좋은 원어민 친구는 내 영어 개인교사가 될 수 있다
____ 돈이 많이 들더라. 원어민 친구 사귀기야 말이야 쉽지 특히 남자인 경우는 외국인 여성들에게 관심 끌기가 솔직히 어려운 게 사실이다. 인정하자.

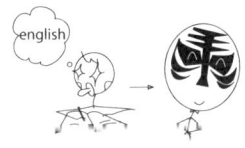

한국에서 영어권 문화를 즐기세요
____ 이태원으로 영어권 문화를 즐기러 갔는데 우리끼리 놀다 왔다. 글고 이태원 솔직히 무섭더라.

미드로 영어 공부를 하세요
____ 못 알아 들으니까 자막만 봤다. 자막 없이 보니까 뭔 말인지 알 수가 없어서 10분 보다 잤다.

영자 신문을 활용해서 영어 공부를 하세요
____ 영자 신문을 읽을 정도면 영어 공부 안한다.

영어로 읽은 내용을 요약해서 정리하세요
____ 재밌군. 읽은 내용이 이해도 안가는 데 요약해서 정리까지 하라. 내 미국친구한테 조선일보 던져주면서 읽고 요약하라고 하면 날 욕하겠지?

영작, 많이 써보면 실력이 향상된다
____ 말했지? 영어 일기 2줄 쓰는 것도 힘들다고…차라리 '미국에 10년 가서 영어 공부하세요' 가 더 설득력 있는 것 같은데. 근데 직장 때려 치고 미국 가서 10년 영어 공부할 동안 체류비는 누가 내주지? 애들 학원비는?

영춘선생이 하고 싶은 말은 이겁니다.

"영어 면접을 준비하는 구직자에게는 1차적 목표로 영어 면접만 대비할 수 있을 만큼의 영어 실력을 갖추면 됩니다. 그 다음 본인의 업무에 맞는 영어를 공부하는 것을 2차 목표로 잡으면 됩니다."

영어 면접을 준비하는 사람이 CNN뉴스 강의를 들어봐야 직접적인 도움이 되지 않습니다. 작년에 한국에서 미드 열풍이 불어 닥쳤을 때 너도 나도 미드를 보며 영어 공부를 하겠다고 했습니다. 영어 왕초보가 백날 미드만 보고 있으면 영어가 어떻게 느는지 누구 하나 진지하게 설명을 해주지 않고 그냥 미드는 흥미와 영어 공부를 동시에 잡을 수 있다고 했습니다.

영어 왕초보가 아무것도 안하고 1년 동안 미드만 보면 아마 영어가 늘겠지만 한국에서 직장인들이나 대학생들에게는 직장 출근이나 학교에 등교하지 않고 미드만 보는 것은 불가능한 일입니다. 영어 하나를 위해 학교와 직장을 나가지 않을 수는 없으니까요.

영어가 늘기 위해서 왕초보들에게 필요한 것은 자신감, 정확하고 이룰 수 있다는 목표 그리고 끈기입니다. 직장 그만두고 영어만 매달리면 영어 못할 사람이 어디 있겠냐 만은 현실적으로 어려운 일입니다. 그래서 영춘선생이 영어 왕초보들에게 제안하는 영어 학습법이 아래의 내용입니다.

영어 말하기를 시작하는 영어 왕초보들은 기본적인 영어 말하기를 1차적인 목표로 세우고 영어를 공부하면 됩니다. 영어 기본단어 300여 단어만 알면 1800여 문장을 구사할 수 있습니다. 결코 많지 않은 양입니다. 이 정도만 목표로 잡고 시작하면 됩니다.

영어로 '리먼 브라더스의 파산'에 관해서 토론을 할 정도를 목표로 잡는다면 다년 장기 계획을 세워야 합니다. (대부분의 한국 사람과 같이 한국에서 영어 공부를 한다는 조건입니다.)

그리고 끈기입니다. 영어를 3개월에 마스터 해서 영어 발표와 영어 토론을 하기는 솔직히 무리입니다. 뭐든지 마찬가지입니다. 포토샵을 배우건 대학 졸업장을 따기 위해 공부를 하건 정해진 기간이 있습니다. 개인적으로 차이가 있을 수 있지만 어느 정도의 기간은 감수해야 합니다.

영어는 공부가 아니고 본인이 의사 표현을 할 수 있는 방법 중 하나입니다. 사랑하는 사람이 있다고 생각해 봅시다. 한국 사람이면 '사랑합니다.' 라고 말하면 되고 미국 사람이면 'I love you' 라고 말하면 됩니다.

영어 말하기는 절대로 공부가 아닙니다. 단순한 의사 표현의 방법 중 하나일 뿐입니다.

Contents

VISUAL VOCA333
Basic

2words
Review
3words
Review
4words
Review
5words
Review
6words
Review

7words   ★13Page
Review   ★103Page
8words   ★115Page
Review   ★201Page
9 words   ★213Page
Review   ★284Page

VISUAL VOCA333
Intermediate

VISUAL VOCA333
Advanced

10words
Review
11words
Review
12 words
Review

Speaking English

using **7 Words**

"7단어로 영어를 말할 수 있어요!"

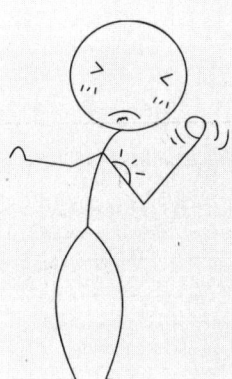

No pain, No English
_Youngchoon

7 Words

001

Found

I found the men jogging very early

002

Man

Do you know that man over there?

003

Seen

I have never seen him here before

I found the men jogging very early 나는 그 남자들이 아주 일찍 조깅하는 것을 발견했다 **Do you know that man over there?** 너는 저기 있는 저 남자 아니? **I have never seen him here before** 나는 전에는 한 번도 여기서 그를 본 적이 없다

004

Very

He gave me a very good example

005

Answer

You must give a better answer then

006

Young

I read a story about young love

He gave me a very good example 그는 나에게 아주 좋은 예를 알려주었다 You must give a better answer then 그때는 네가 더 나은 답을 내놓아야 할거다 I read a story about young love 나는 젊은 사랑에 대한 이야기를 읽었다

007

Last

He was at the ball last night

008

Not

He is not that good for me

009

To

Will you come with me to Korea?

He was at the ball last night 그는 지난밤 무도회에 있었다 **He is not that good for me** 그는 나에게 그렇게 도움이 안 된다 **Will you come with me to Korea?** 나와 함께 한국에 갈래?

010

Where

Where did you get that short story?

011

My

My best friend gave it to me

012

Money

I found some money under the table

Where did you get that short story? 그 짧은 이야기를 어디에서 들었니? **My best friend gave it to me** 나의 가장 친한 친구가 그것을 주었다 **I found some money under the table** 나는 탁자 밑에서 돈을 좀 찾았다

013

It

I still have to think about it

014

Parents

I will talk with your parents today

015

If

It is better if we both do

I still have to think about it 나는 여전히 그것에 관해 생각해야 한다 **I will talk with your parents today** 나는 오늘 너의 부모님과 이야기할 것이다 **It is better if we both do** 우리 둘 다 한다면 더 좋을 것이다

The children must have left it there 그 아이들이 그것을 거기에 두고 온 것이 틀림없다
What do you think about that man? 그 남자에 대해서 어떻게 생각하니? I think he is not good enough 나는 그가 충분히 괜찮지 않다고 생각한다

019

Mother

Mother and father will come over today

020

Tell

Tell them to bring something for us

021

Bring

I will tell them to bring food

Mother and father will come over today 어머니와 아버지가 오늘 오실 것이다 **Tell them to bring something for us** 그들에게 우릴 위해 무엇인가 가져오라고 말해라 **I will tell them to bring food** 나는 그들에게 음식을 가져오라고 말할 것이다

Who can do the show better then? 그럼 누가 그 쇼를 더 잘할 수 있을까? **No one does it better than me** 나보다 그것을 더 잘할 수 있는 사람은 아무도 없다 **Do you know where his car is?** 너는 그의 차가 어디에 있는지 아니?

I will come home early from school 나는 학교에서 집에 일찍 올 것이다 Where did you see the three children? 어디서 그 세 명의 아이들을 보았니? I saw them jogging at the park 나는 그들이 공원에서 조깅하는 것을 보았다

I saw it behind that old house 나는 그것이 그 오래된 집 뒤에 있는 것을 보았다
Are you sure you saw it there? 너는 거기서 그것을 본 게 확실해? Several people tried to leave the city 몇몇 사람들은 그 도시를 떠나려고 노력했다

031

Later

I will leave for the city later

032

Next

I will see you again next time

033

Over

Those children over there can jump high

I will leave for the city later 나는 나중에 그 도시로 떠날 것이다 **I will see you again next time** 나는 너를 다음번에 또 볼 것이다 **Those children over there can jump high** 저기 저 아이들은 높이 뛰어오를 수 있다

034

Often

His friend often writes him a letter

035

Room

Many children go dancing in the room

036

Many

Many people talked about the funny man

His friend often writes him a letter 그의 친구는 종종 그에게 편지를 쓴다 Many children go dancing in the room 많은 아이들이 방에서 춤을 추러 간다 Many people talked about the funny man 많은 사람들이 그 재미있는 남자에 대해서 이야기했다

I want to see them in school 나는 그들을 학교에서 보고 싶다 **My mother brought some food for me** 나의 어머니가 나를 위해 약간의 음식을 가져왔다 **I think that is enough for us** 나는 그것이 우리를 위해 충분하다고 생각한다

Most people wish for a big house 대부분의 사람들이 큰 집을 바란다   One important thing in life is money 인생에서 중요한 한 가지는 돈이다   She might be late for the show 그녀는 쇼에 늦을 수도 있다

043 Writes — She writes a letter to her mother

044 Not — I do not do that very often

045 Ball — I went to the ball with him

She writes a letter to her mother 그녀는 어머니에게 편지를 쓴다 **I do not do that very often** 나는 그것을 아주 자주 하지는 않는다 **I went to the ball with him** 나는 그와 함께 무도회에 갔다

046 Group — The child often walks with the group

047 Some — It may mean love to some people

048 Start — Is it enough to start right here?

The child often walks with the group 그 아이는 종종 그 무리와 함께 걷는다 **It may mean love to some people** 그것은 어떤 사람들에게는 사랑을 의미할 수도 있다 **Is it enough to start right here?** 바로 여기에서 출발하면 충분해?

049 **Just** — What you just said was really funny

050 **Why** — Why do you want to do this?

051 **Something** — It is important to do something different

What you just said was really funny 네가 방금 말한 것은 정말 재미있었다 **Why do you want to do this?** 너는 왜 이걸 하고 싶어? **It is important to do something different** 무엇인가 다른 것을 하는 게 중요하다

She thought she knew what she wanted 그녀는 자신이 무엇을 원하는지 알고 있다고 생각했다
He knew his letter had not come 그는 그의 편지가 도착하지 않았다는 것을 알았다
He tried to stop her from crying 그는 그녀가 우는 것을 멈추게 하려고 노력했다

055 **That** — How come she left with that man?

056 **Mean** — Hope and love mean a great life

057 **Seven** — She was jogging from seven to nine

How come she left with that man? 어째서 그녀가 그 남자와 함께 떠났지? **Hope and love mean a great life** 희망과 사랑은 훌륭한 삶을 의미한다 **She was jogging from seven to nine** 그녀는 일곱 시부터 아홉 시까지 조깅을 했다

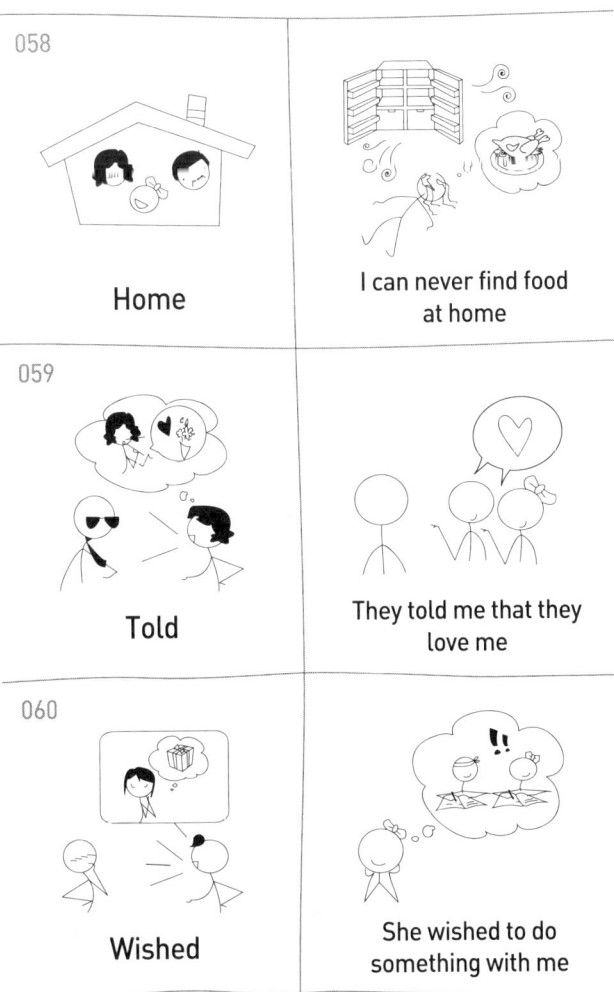

I can never find food at home 나는 집에서 결코 음식을 찾을 수 없다 They told me that they love me 그들은 나를 사랑한다고 말했다 She wished to do something with me 그녀는 나와 함께 무엇인가 하기를 바랐다

061

If

Do it, if it is something important

062

Man

The old smiling man is my father

063

Move

We must make our move early on

Do it, if it is something important 그것이 중요한 것이라면 그것을 해라 The old smiling man is my father 그 웃고 있는 나이든 남자가 나의 아버지다 We must make our move early on 우리는 일찍부터 움직여야 한다

064

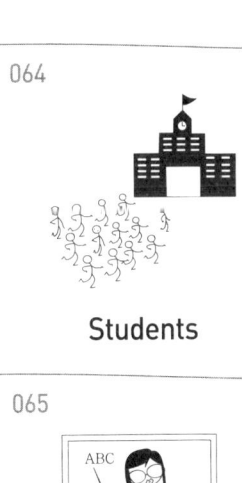

Students

They saw you together with the students

065

Learn

The students wanted to learn with them

066

Car

The body of his car is great

They saw you together with the students 그들은 네가 그 학생들과 함께 있는 것을 보았다 **The students wanted to learn with them** 그 학생들은 그들과 함께 공부하기를 원했다 **The body of his car is great** 그의 자동차의 몸체는 훌륭하다

067

Each

Each mother asked about something really important

068

Funny

What you said was funny to them

069

Long

She gave him a long letter today

Each mother asked about something really important 각 어머니들은 정말 중요한 무엇인가에 대해 물었다 **What you said was funny to them** 네가 말한 것이 그들에게 재미있었다 **She gave him a long letter today** 그녀는 오늘 그에게 긴 편지를 주었다

070 Nine — Only nine students are listening to me

071 And — My family and I never eat together

072 Now — What are you listening to right now?

Only nine students are listening to me 단지 아홉 명의 학생들만 나의 말을 듣고 있다
My family and I never eat together 가족과 나는 절대 함께 식사하지 않는다   **What are you listening to right now?** 바로 지금 무엇을 듣고 있니?

073
Also

The teacher also asked them to wait

074
Try

Each boy gave dancing a good try

075
Name

My name must sound really funny here

The teacher also asked them to wait 그 교사는 또한 그들에게 기다리라고 요청했다
Each boy gave dancing a good try 각각의 소년이 춤을 한번 좋게 시도해 보았다
My name must sound really funny here 나의 이름은 이곳에서 아주 웃기게 들릴 것이 틀림없다

076

Like

Do you like jogging in the park?

077

About

What can you say about his children?

078

This

She and I started jogging from today

Do you like jogging in the park? 공원에서 조깅하는 것을 좋아하니? What can you say about his children? 너는 그의 아이들에 대해 뭐라고 말할 수 있니? She and I started jogging from today 그녀와 나는 오늘부터 조깅을 시작하였다

079	
Idea	The idea came to him one morning
080	
When	People started smiling when they saw me
081	
Say	I kind of heard her say that

The idea came to him one morning 어느 날 아침 그 생각이 그에게 떠올랐다
People started smiling when they saw me 사람들이 나를 볼 때면 웃기 시작했다
I kind of heard her say that 나는 그녀가 그렇게 말하는 걸 좀 들었다

082

Who

Who called me after I left home?

083

Door

Why did you close the back door?

084

Do

Do not let the children go out

Who called me after I left home? 내가 집을 나선 뒤에 누가 전화했어? **Why did you close the back door?** 너는 왜 뒷문을 닫았니? **Do not let the children go out** 아이들을 나가게 하지 말아라

085

Shown

She has not shown her face here

086

Without

She could not play without her friend

087

She

I know what she did last night

She has not shown her face here 그녀는 이곳에서 얼굴을 보여주지 않았다 **She could not play without her friend** 그녀는 친구들 없이는 놀 수 없었다 **I know what she did last night** 나는 그녀가 지난 밤에 무엇을 하였는지 안다

The parents also laughed at the idea 부모님들 또한 그 아이디어를 비웃었다 How do you make your room warm? 어떻게 너의 방을 따뜻하게 만드니? I saw an old friend last night 나는 지난 밤 옛 친구를 보았다

I know what she said to him 나는 그녀가 그에게 뭐라고 말했는지 안다 **The big group of students must come** 학생들의 큰 무리가 와야 한다 **It is so hot in your room** 너의 방 안은 너무 덥다

Her mean boyfriend has a great body 그녀의 비열한 남자친구는 훌륭한 신체를 가졌다
They heard something in the small room 그들은 작은 방에서 무엇인가를 들었다
His dancing girlfriend has a great body 그의 춤추는 여자친구는 훌륭한 신체를 가졌다

097

Night

There are a few people at night

098

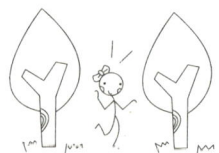

Between

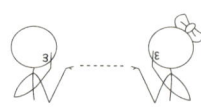

This must be between you and me

099

Their

They left their old car to us

There are a few people at night 밤에는 소수의 사람들이 있다 **This must be between you and me** 이건 너와 나 사이의 비밀이야야 한다 **They left their old car to us** 그들은 낡은 자동차를 우리에게 남겼다

100

Writes

She writes a good story about Youngchoon

101

Sun

The sun brought light to the room

102

Second

She is the second in their class

She writes a good story about Youngchoon 그녀는 영춘에 관한 훌륭한 이야기를 쓴다
The sun brought light to the room 태양이 그 방 안에 빛을 가져왔다 She is the second in their class 그녀는 그들의 학급에서 2등이다

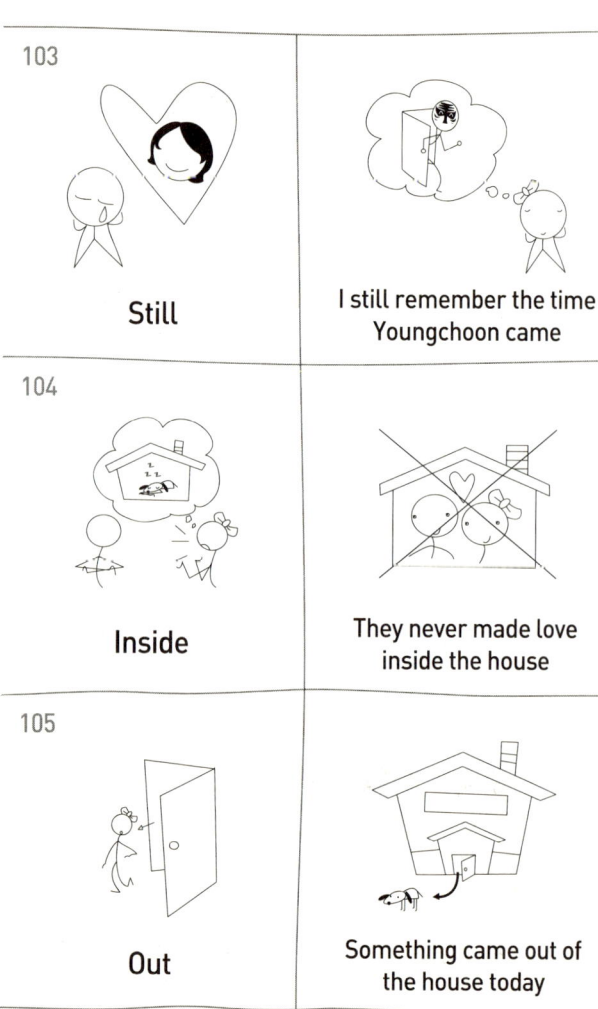

103
Still
I still remember the time Youngchoon came

104
Inside
They never made love inside the house

105
Out
Something came out of the house today

I still remember the time Youngchoon came 나는 아직도 영춘이 왔던 때를 기억한다
They never made love inside the house 그들은 집 안에서는 결코 사랑을 나누지 않았다 **Something came out of the house today** 오늘 집에서 무엇인가 나왔다

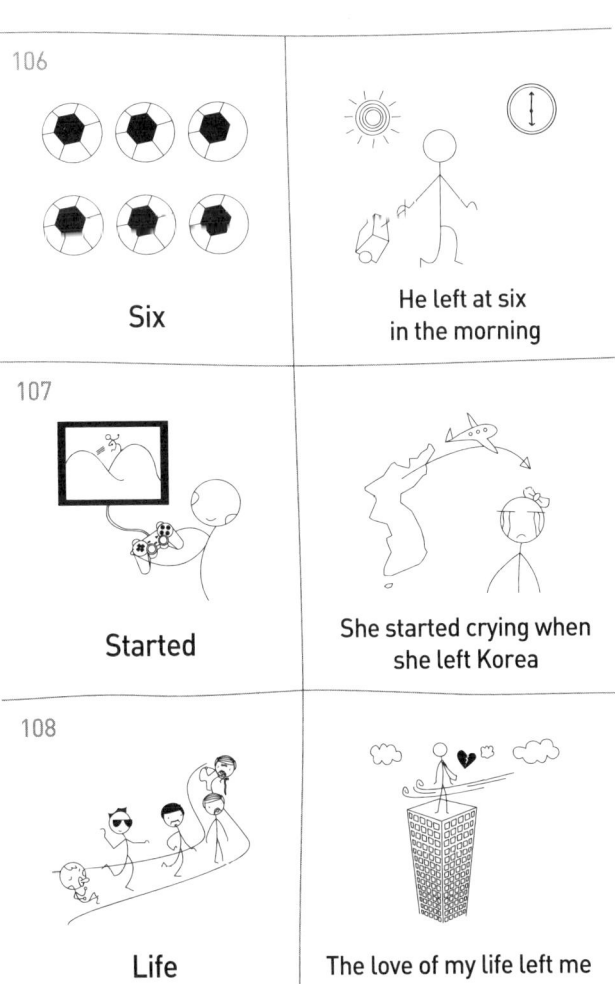

106

Six

He left at six in the morning

107

Started

She started crying when she left Korea

108

Life

The love of my life left me

He left at six in the morning 그는 아침 여섯 시에 떠났다   **She started crying when she left Korea** 그녀는 한국을 떠날 때 울기 시작했다   **The love of my life left me** 나의 인생의 사랑이 떠났다

He gave me a ride to school 그가 나를 학교에 태워다 주었다 **I also want to tell you something** 나 또한 너에게 무엇인가 말하고 싶다 **You can not just leave me out** 너는 그냥 날 이렇게 빼돌수 없다

What time will your class end today? 오늘 수업이 몇 시에 끝나니? **She was kind to the old man** 그녀는 그 노인에게 친절했다 **The king of this country is mean** 이 나라의 왕은 비열하다

115 Body — I want to have a great body

116 Too — It is too late for that now

117 Made — You made me what I am today

I want to have a great body 나는 훌륭한 몸을 가지고 싶다 **It is too late for that now** 이제 그것을 하기에는 너무 늦었다 **You made me what I am today** 네가 오늘의 나를 만들었다

118

Walks

The man in green walks very fast

119

An

The big boy is an only child

120

Run

Children in my class can run fast

The man in green walks very fast 녹색 옷의 남자가 매우 빠르게 걷는다 The big boy is an only child 그 커다란 아이는 외동이다 Children in my class can run fast 우리 반 아이들은 빨리 달릴 수 있다

I was about to tell her something 나는 막 무언가를 말하려던 참이었다 **He came to me and asked something** 그가 나에게 와서 무언가를 물었다 **They wanted to see the school teacher** 그들은 학교 선생님을 만나고 싶어했다

Our house is far from the city 우리의 집은 도시에서 멀다 She will not remember who we are 그녀는 우리가 누구인지 기억하지 못할 것이다 Her mother is an example to us 그녀의 어머니는 우리에게 본보기였다

127

Second

I am the second in the family

128

With

What did you do with his letter?

129

Inside

I saw the child inside the room

I am the second in the family 나는 가족 중 둘째다 **What did you do with his letter?** 그의 편지를 어떻게 했니? **I saw the child inside the room** 나는 그 아이를 방 안에서 보았다

The show last night was very funny 지난 밤의 쇼는 아주 재미있었다 There were many people in the park 공원에 사람이 많았다 I did not know you were there 네가 거기에 있는지 몰랐다

133

Different

My idea is very different from his

134

Went

The child went out with his mother

135

Three

The three men asked for his money

My idea is very different from his 나의 생각은 그와 아주 다르다 **The child went out with his mother** 아이는 어머니와 함께 나갔다 **The three men asked for his money** 그 세 명의 남자가 그의 돈을 요구했다

136

Family

Her family will go to the city

137

School

My school is far from my house

138

Life

My life will be better without you

Her family will go to the city 그녀의 가족은 그 도시로 갈 것이다 **My school is far from my house** 나의 학교는 집에서 멀다 **My life will be better without you** 네가 없으면 내 삶은 더 나아질 것이다

139
Mean — I did not mean what I said

140
End — I want this day to end now

141
Means — The look in her eyes means something

I did not mean what I said 내가 말한 것은 진심이 아니었다 **I want this day to end now** 이 날이 지금 끝나면 좋겠다 **The look in her eyes means something** 그녀의 눈에 떠오른 표정은 무엇인가를 의미한다

The city is very far from here 그 도시는 여기부터 아주 멀다 The city is not far from here 그 도시는 여기에서 멀지 않다 Only a few students go to school 아주 적은 수의 학생들만이 그 학교에 간다

145

They

Did they really run after your friend?

146

Six

There are six men inside the house

147

Both

Both his parents talked to his teacher

Did they really run after your friend? 그들이 정말로 네 친구를 뒤쫓았니?   There are six men inside the house 그 집 안에 여섯 명의 남자가 있다   Both his parents talked to his teacher 그의 부모님 두 분 다 그의 선생님과 이야기했다

148

Walks

My high school teacher walks very fast

149

Read

It is important to read the story

150

Car

She left her money in the car

My high school teacher walks very fast 나의 고등학교 선생님은 매우 빨리 걷는다
It is important to read the story 그 이야기를 읽는 것이 중요하다   She left her money in the car 그녀는 돈을 차에 두었다

151

Youngchoon

The teacher at Youngchoon is the best

152

You

I called to say I love you

153

For

It is time for us to eat

The teacher at Youngchoon is the best 영춘에 있는 선생님이 최고다 **I called to say I love you** 나는 너를 사랑한다고 말하기 위해 전화했다 **It is time for us to eat** 우리가 식사할 시간이다

154 Must	You must write a letter for her
155 Only	Only a few knew the right answer
156 Call	I waited for his call last night

You must write a letter for her 너는 그녀를 위해 편지를 써야 한다 Only a few knew the right answer 아주 적은 수많이 정확한 답을 알았다 I waited for his call last night 나는 지난 밤 그의 전화를 기다렸다

7words

The children are dancing in the park 그 아이들이 공원에서 춤을 추고 있는 중이다 Our group brought a big green tree 우리 무리는 커다란 녹색 나무를 가져왔다
Six small children are making her leave 여섯 명의 작은 아이들이 그녀를 떠나게 만들었다

A group of six men helped us 여섯 명의 남자들 무리가 우리를 도왔다 **You know what I want to know** 너는 내가 무엇을 알고 싶어하는지 안다 **You know what I want from you** 너는 내가 무엇을 원하는지 안다

163
Here

Can we just wait for him here?

164
Time

Do you still have time for her?

165
Love

I will never ever look for love

Can we just wait for him here? 그냥 여기서 그를 기다려도 돼? **Do you still have time for her?** 아직 그녀를 만날 시간이 있니? **I will never ever look for love** 나는 결코 사랑을 찾지 않을 것이다

166

Paper

He writes something on his green paper

167

Tried

We tried but could not know more

168

People

Many people often say I look good

He writes something on his green paper 그는 녹색 종이에 무엇인가를 쓴다 We tried but could not know more 우리는 노력했지만 더 알아낼 수 없었다 Many people often say I look good 많은 사람들이 종종 내가 좋아 보인다고 말한다

169
Sure — I am sure love will find me

170
Cold — It was very cold in their room

171
Eat — I really want to eat something cold

I am sure love will find me 나는 사랑이 나를 찾아올 거라고 확신한다 **It was very cold in their room** 나는 그들의 방에서 매우 추웠다 **I really want to eat something cold** 나는 뭔가 차가운 것이 정말 먹고 싶다

172

Father

My father died inside an old house

173

But

The boy is not intelligent but funny

174

Late

The boy came to class really late

My father died inside an old house 나의 아버지가 낡은 집안에서 돌아가셨다 **The boy is not intelligent but funny** 그 소년은 지적이지 않지만 매우 재미있다 **The boy came to class really late** 그 소년은 수업에 정말 늦게 왔다

175

Kept

I kept his letter in my room

176

Early

His father died early in the morning

177

Teacher

My new teacher has a big family

I kept his letter in my room 나는 그의 편지를 내 방에 두었다 **His father died early in the morning** 그의 아버지는 아침 일찍 돌아가셨다 **My new teacher has a big family** 나의 새로운 선생님은 식구가 많다

178

Helped

Have you helped her with the story?

179

So

The five dancing children look so funny

180

End

My love for him will never end

Have you helped her with the story? 그녀가 그 이야기 하는 것을 네가 도왔니? **The five dancing children look so funny** 춤추는 다섯 명의 아이들은 정말 우습게 보인다 **My love for him will never end** 그에 대한 나의 사랑은 절대 끝나지 않을 것이다

7words

181
Warm

I could still feel his warm hand

182
Day

He writes to me every other day

183
Hour

The show will start in an hour

I could still feel his warm hand 나는 여전히 그의 따뜻한 손을 느낄 수 있다 **He writes to me every other day** 그는 이틀에 한 번씩 내게 편지를 쓴다 **The show will start in an hour** 쇼가 한 시간 내로 시작할 것이다

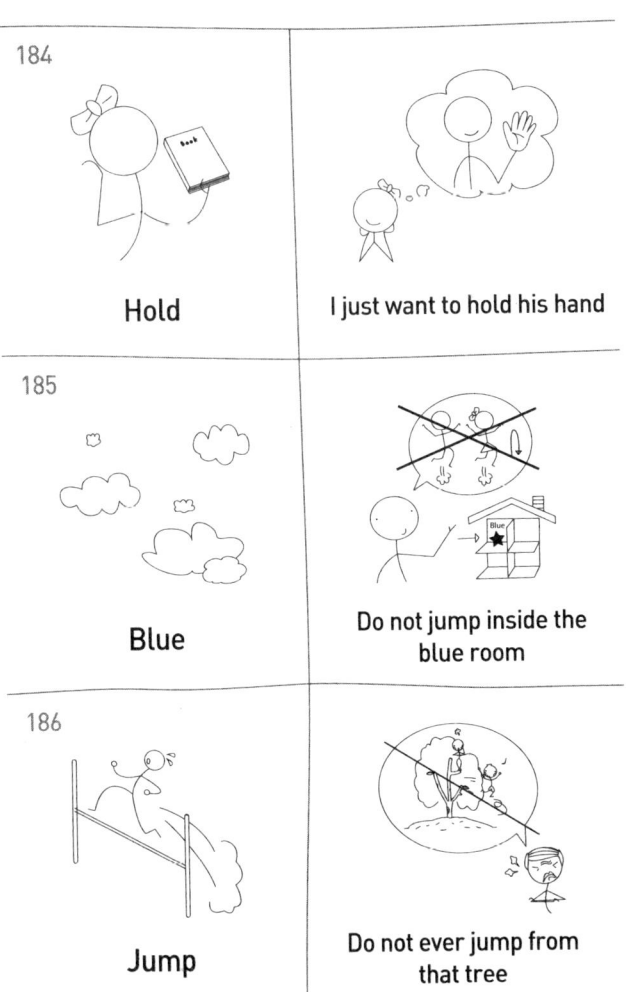

184
Hold

I just want to hold his hand

185
Blue

Do not jump inside the blue room

186
Jump

Do not ever jump from that tree

I just want to hold his hand 나는 다만 그의 손을 잡고 싶다 **Do not jump inside the blue room** 그 파란 방 안에서는 뛰지 말아라 **Do not ever jump from that tree** 저 나무에서 뛰어내 리지 말아라

187 Up

He was crying after our break up

188 Shown

What you have shown was not enough

189 Ball

I saw them dancing at the ball

He was crying after our break up 그는 우리의 이별 후에 울고 있었다 What you have shown was not enough 네가 보여준 것은 충분하지 않다 I saw them dancing at the ball 나는 그들이 무도회에서 춤추는 것을 보았다

I want to get close to you 나는 너와 가까워지고 싶다 Will you just stop listening to us? 그냥 우리에게 귀 기울이는 것을 그만둬줄래? Did you really make love with him? 너는 정말로 그와 사랑을 나누었니?

May

May I come to your house today?

Was

Our house was on fire last night

Some

He left some food on the table

May I come to your house today? 오늘 너희 집에 가도 돼? Our house was on fire last night 지난밤 우리 집에 불이 났다 He left some food on the table 그는 탁자 위에 음식을 좀 남겨두었다

I want to go to your class 너희 반에 가고 싶다 **I did not mean what I said** 내가 말한 것은 진심이 아니었다 **Do not let them see you crying** 그들이 네가 우는 것을 보게 하지 말아라

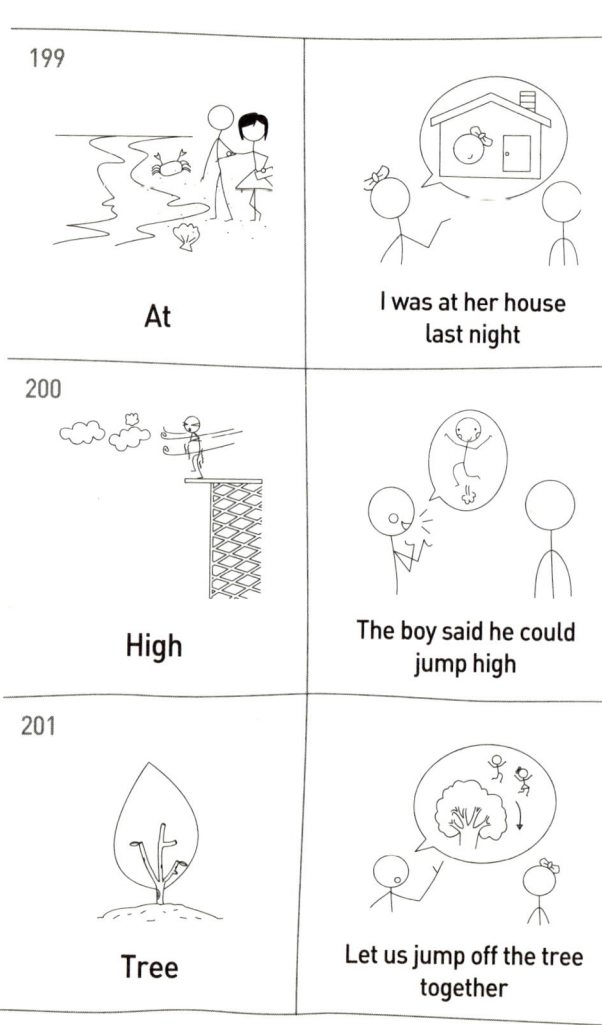

199	
At	I was at her house last night
200	
High	The boy said he could jump high
201	
Tree	Let us jump off the tree together

I was at her house last night 나는 지난 밤 그녀의 집에 있었다 **The boy said he could jump high** 그 소년은 높이 뛸 수 있다고 말했다 **Let us jump off the tree together** 우리 그 나무에서 함께 뛰어내리자

I have to give it a try 나는 그것을 한 번 시도해봐야 한다 I do not want to be here 나는 여기 있고 싶지 않다 I have given you so much love 나는 너에게 아주 많은 사랑을 주었다

The old man spoke to my parents 그 노인이 나의 부모님께 말했다 Those children can jump from that tree 저 아이들은 저 나무에서 뛸수 있다 There is something off in his dancing 그의 춤에는 뭔가 빠진 것이 있다

I do not go with mean people 나는 비열한 사람들과 어울리지 않는다 **Can I go with you to Korea?** 너와 함께 한국에 갈 수 있을까? **We were together for a long time** 우리는 오랫동안 함께있었다

211
Had

He wished he had never seen her

212
Break

A break is what the children wanted

213
Several

Several people said they wanted to talk

He wished he had never seen her 그는 그녀를 본 적이 없었으면 좋겠다고 바랐다
A break is what the children wanted 휴식은 그 아이들이 원했던 것이다 Several people said they wanted to talk 몇몇 사람들은 이야기하기를 원한다고 말했다

Do not give me that funny look 내게 그런 웃기는 표정 짓지 말아라 I just want to start making money 나는 다만 돈을 벌기 시작하기를 원한다 He gave me a long love letter 그는 나에게 긴 연애 편지를 보냈다.

217

Bring

I will bring you to my house

218

In

I really want to live in Korea

219

Hour

I have to go in an hour

I will bring you to my house 나는 너를 집으로 데려올 것이다 **I really want to live in Korea** 나는 정말 한국에서 살고 싶다 **I have to go in an hour** 나는 한 시간 내에 가야 한다

220

Important

My parents are very important to me

221

We

We have to look for better means

222

Means

It means we have to do better

My parents are very important to me 나의 부모님은 나에게 매우 중요하다 **We have to look for better means** 우리는 더 나은 방법을 찾아야 한다 **It means we have to do better** 그것은 우리가 더 잘 해야 한다는 것을 뜻한다

Can your parents look after her today? 너의 부모님이 오늘 그녀를 돌봐줄 수 있니?
I have a good idea about this 내게 이것에 대해 좋은 생각이 있다 **He has a blue and black ball** 그는 푸르고 검은 공을 가졌다

226

Youngchoon

The boy asked his mother about Youngchoon

227

Mother

I have to help my mother today

228

Your

How can you help your mother today?

The boy asked his mother about Youngchoon 그 소년이 어머니에게 영춘에 관해 물었다 **I have to help my mother today** 나는 오늘 어머니를 도와야 한다 **How can you help your mother today?** 너는 어떻게 오늘 어머니를 도울 수 있니?

229

Our

The children are smiling at our parents

230

Short

I have a short but good story

231

Also

I also want to be with you

The children are smiling at our parents 그 아이들은 우리 부모님에게 미소 짓고 있다
I have a short but good story 나에게 짧지만 좋은 이야기가 있다 **I also want to be with you** 나도 너와 함께있고 싶다

I will go to the big house 나는 그 큰 집에 갈 것이다 She will go to the big house 그녀는 그 큰 집에 갈 것이다 I kept the love letter from her 나는 그녀가 보낸 연애 편지를 간직했다

235

Heard

My friend heard me crying this morning

236

Jump

We have to jump first before dancing

237

Second

My father is at the second table

My friend heard me crying this morning 나의 친구는 오늘 아침 내가 우는 것을 들었다
We have to jump first before dancing 우리는 춤추기 전에 먼저 뛰어야 한다
My father is at the second table 나의 아버지는 두 번째 탁자에 계신다

Did you mean what you just said? 너 방금 한 말 진심이니? **I did not mean to say that** 그렇게 말할 생각은 아니었다 **He started to speak like a king** 그는 왕처럼 말하기 시작했다

241 **Learn** — When will you start to learn dancing?

242 **Big** — Do not show me your big eyes!

243 **So** — Why do you look so blue today?

When will you start to learn dancing? 너는 언제 춤을 배우기 시작할 거니? **Do not show me your big eyes!** 내게 너의 큰 눈을 보이지 마래! **Why do you look so blue today?** 너 오늘 왜 그렇게 우울해 보여?

244

Live

My parents live next to my teacher

245

Child

The kind man helped the crying child

246

Ball

The child asked for a blue ball

My parents live next to my teacher 나의 부모님들은 나의 선생님 이웃에 산다 The kind man helped the crying child 그 친절한 남자는 울고 있는 아이를 도왔다 The child asked for a blue ball 그 아이는 파란색 공을 요구했다

247 **Get** — How can I get in my house?

248 **How** — How often do you call your friend?

249 **Make** — How did your mother make this food?

How can I get in my house? 나 어떻게 나의 집에 들어가지? **How often do you call your friend?** 너는 친구들에게 얼마나 자주 전화하니? **How did your mother make this food?** 너의 어머니는 어떻게 이 음식을 만들었니?

Close your eyes and hold my hand 눈을 감고 내 손을 잡아라 Something about this house is not right 이 집에 관한 무엇인가가 잘못되었다 Are you ready to run after me? 너는 나를 쫓을 준비가 되었니?

253

Who

Who is the boy next to you?

254

We

We will be attending the show today

255

Number

Number nine is a very good number

Who is the boy next to you? 너의 옆에 있는 소년은 누구니? **We will be attending the show today** 우리는 오늘 쇼를 보러 갈 것이다 **Number nine is a very good number** 숫자9는 좋은 숫자다

Which teacher has shown the best example? 어떤 선생님이 가장 좋은 예를 보여줬나? **I want to have that car, too** 나도 그 차를 가지고 싶다 **I will make it to the top** 나는 정상에 오를 것이다

259

Father

Her father kept listening to his mother

260

Important

Korea is really important to the people

261

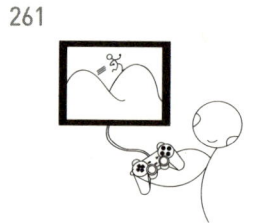

Started

He started to help the parents today

Her father kept listening to his mother 그녀의 아버지는 그의 어머니에게 계속 귀를 기울였다
Korea is really important to the people 한국은 국민들에게 정말 중요하다 He started to
help the parents today 그는 오늘 부모님을 돕기 시작했다

262

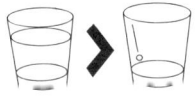

Much

He means so much to my family

263

Boy

Do you remember the funny, intelligent boy?

264

Those

Do not be mean to those children

He means so much to my family 그는 나의 가족에게 매우 큰 의미가 있다 Do you remember the funny, intelligent boy? 재미있고 똑똑한 그 소년을 기억하니? Do not be mean to those children 저 아이들에게 심술궂게 굴지 말아라

7 Words
Review

영춘선생이 알려주는 Review 활용법!

1. 그림과 문장을 보고 의미를 파악합니다
되도록이면 해석을 보지 않고 영어 그대로의
의미를 파악하도록 노력하세요!

2. MP3로 Review 부분을 들으면서 네이티브들의 정확한 발음을 청취합니다
네이티브들의 문장은 두 번씩 반복 됩니다.
처음에는 발음을 청취를 하고 두 번째는 조용히 따라 읽습니다.

3. 이제 Review 부분을 큰 소리 내어 읽습니다
영어는 마음속에 담아두기 위해 배우는 언어가 아닙니다.
마음껏 소리치면서 읽으세요!
단, 전철이나 버스 같은 대중교통에서 책을 읽으시는 분들은
주위 사람들에게 피해가 가지 않게 특별히 조심해 주세요!

★주로 대중교통을 이용하는 영춘선생이 이 책을 들고 다니시는 분을 뵙게 되면 친필 싸인을 즉시 제공하겠습니다.

Review

→ 002

Do you know that man over there?

013 ←

I still have to think about it

→ 003

I have never seen him here before

019 ←

Mother and father will come over today

→ 009

Will you come with me to Korea?

025 ←

I will come home early from school

→ 093

It is so hot in your room

072 ←

What are you listening to right now?

→ 098

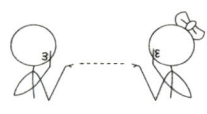

This must be between you and me

076 ←

Do you like jogging in the park?

→ 071

My family and I never eat together

082 ←

Who called me after I left home?

→ 109

He gave me a ride to school

133 ←

My idea is very different from his

→ 115

I want to have a great body

153 ←

It is time for us to eat

→ 127

I am the second in the family

112 ←

What time will your class end today?

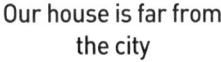

Our house is far from the city

Her family will go to the city

There were many people in the park

My school is far from my house

I did not know you were there

The city is very far from here

→ 164

Do you still have time for her?

182 ←

He writes to me every other day

→ 170

It was very cold in their room

183 ←

The show will start in an hour

→ 171

I really want to eat something cold

193 ←

May I come to your house today?

→ 195

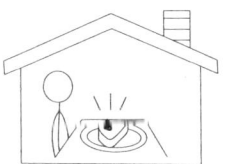

He left some food on the table

203 ←

I do not want to be here

→ 199

I was at her house last night

209 ←

Can I go with you to Korea?

→ 168

Many people often say I look good

214 ←

Do not give me that funny look

→ 217

I will bring you to my house

224 ←

I have a good idea about this

→ 218

I really want to live in Korea

231 ←

I also want to be with you

→ 219

I have to go in an hour

243 ←

Why do you look so blue today?

Speaking English

using 8 Words

8단어로 영어를 말할 수 있어요!"

죽어라 영어 공부해도
진짜 죽지는 않는다 _영춘선생

8 Words

001

But

I called her but she did not answer

002

Then

I think she was still at school then

003

Every

I love jogging with my students every morning

I called her but she did not answer 나의 그녀에게 전화를 걸었지만 받지 않았다
I think she was still at school then 나는 그때 그녀가 여전히 학교에 다닌다고 생각했다 I love jogging with my students every morning 나는 나의 학생들과 매일 아침 조깅하는 것을 즐긴다

004

High

But, there is only one high school here

005

Even

Even so, our school is still the best

006

Better

He had better move to a new house

But, there is only one high school here 하지만, 여기에는 고등학교가 하나밖에 없다 Even so, our school is still the best 그렇다고 하더라도, 우리 학교가 여전히 최고다 He had better move to a new house 그는 새로운 집으로 이사 가는 편이 낫다

Have you ever tried jogging at the park? 이제까지 공원에서 조깅해본 적 있니?
You may look for me or my mother 당신은 나나 나의 어머니를 찾을 수 있을 것이다
Is she really your mother or your friend? 그녀는 정말 너의 어머니 아니면 너의 친구니?

010 Keep — Just keep it inside and then move on

011 How — How do I know if it is right?

012 Attending — Are you sure you are still attending school?

Just keep it inside and then move on 그냥 그걸 안에 놔두고 출발해 How do I know if it is right? 그것이 맞는지 내가 어떻게 알지? Are you sure you are still attending school? 너는 여전히 학교 다니는 게 확실해?

013

Thank

Say "Thank you" to those who helped you

014

Children

You are very different from the children here

015

Sentence

Make a sentence about a mother and child

Say "Thank you" to those who helped you 너를 도와준 사람들에게 "고마워"라고 말해라
You are very different from the children here 너는 여기 아이들과 아주 다르다 **Make a sentence about a mother and child** 엄마와 아이에 대한 문장을 만들어라

The child has asked his parents about love 그 아이는 부모님에게 사랑에 대해 물었다
They just laughed and talked with each other 그들은 그냥 서로 웃고 떠들었다 **Have you ever given your friend a ride?** 이제까지 네 친구들을 태워준 적이 있니?

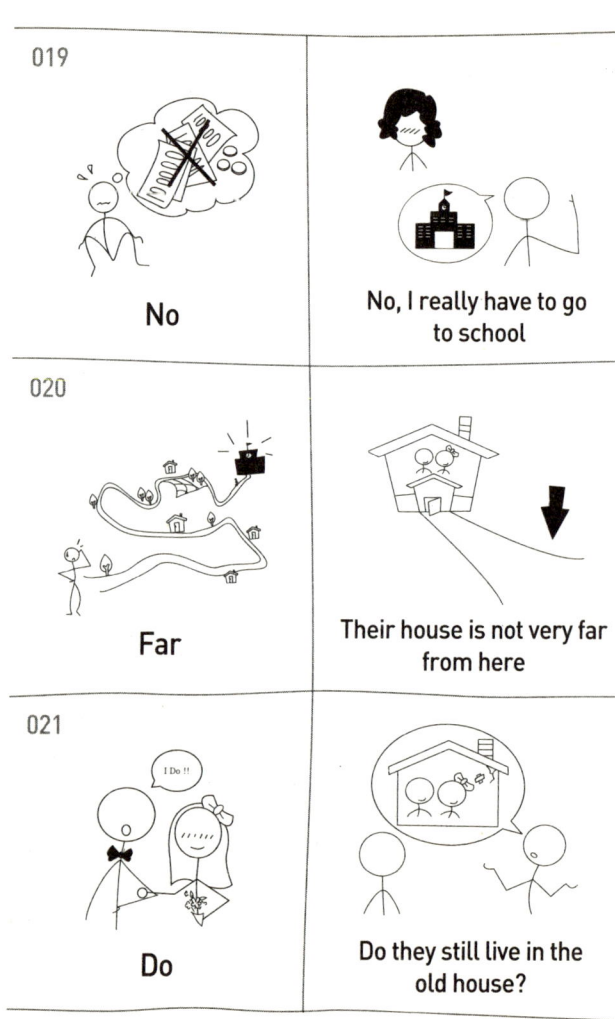

No, I really have to go to school 아니, 난 정말로 학교에 가야 한다 **Their house is not very far from here** 그들의 집은 여기에서 많이 멀지 않다 **Do they still live in the old house?** 그들은 여전히 그 낡은 집에 사니?

022

Am

I am sure that life will get better

023

Ever

Have you ever wished not to be blue?

024

Eyes

Your little eyes make me feel really good

I am sure that life will get better 난 삶이 더 나아질 거라고 확신한다 **Have you ever wished not to be blue?** 이제까지 우울하지 않았으면 하고 바란 적 있어? **Your little eyes make me feel really good** 네 작은 눈이 나를 정말 기분 좋게 만든다

I think I heard her crying last night 나는 지난 밤 그녀가 우는 소리를 들었다고 생각한다 The boy asked me to make a sentence 그 소년이 내게 문장 하나를 만들어달라고 요청했다 What took you so long to come back? 무엇이 네가 이렇게 늦게 돌아오도록 했니?

028

Men

Many old men try to look so young

029

Jogging

I saw them jogging together in the morning

030

Name

Each name was called out from the group

Many old men try to look so young 많은 노인들이 매우 젊게 보이려고 애쓴다
I saw them jogging together in the morning 나는 아침에 그들이 함께 조깅하는 것을 보았다
Each name was called out from the group 각각의 이름은 그 무리에서 호명되었다

I waited for him to say thank you 나는 고맙다고 말하려고 그를 기다렸다 **I just hope you got what you wanted** 나는 다만 네가 원하던 것을 얻었기를 바란다 **Is she the first or the second child?** 그녀는 첫째 아이니 둘째 아이니?

034

Jump

Do you close your eyes as you jump?

035

Several

I have seen her talk with several men

036

Face

I have never seen a face too small

Do you close your eyes as you jump? 너는 뛸 때 눈을 감니? I have seen her talk with several men 나는 그녀가 몇몇 남자들과 이야기하는 것을 보았다 I have never seen a face too small 나는 너무 작은 얼굴을 한번도 본 적이 없다

037

Family

She is the second child in the family

038

City

There was a big fire in the city

039

Fire

Do you know what time the fire started?

She is the second child in the family 그녀는 그 가족의 둘째 아이다 **There was a big fire in the city** 시내에 큰 불이 났다 **Do you know what time the fire started?** 불이 몇 시에 시작 됐는지 알고 있니?

040

No

Inside the house, no one made a sound

041

He

He gave me a ride with his car

042

Or

Do you want a car or a house?

Inside the house, no one made a sound 집 안에서는 아무도 소리를 내지 않았다
He gave me a ride with his car 그가 그의 자동차로 나를 태워 주었다 Do you want a car or a house? 너는 자동차를 원하니 아니면 집을 원하니?

I have asked even my mother about that 나는 우리 엄마에게 조차 그것에 대해 물었다 Did he say something before he left today? 그가 오늘 떠나기 전에 무엇인가 말했느냐? He just left a letter on the table 그는 단지 탁자 위에 편지 한 장을 남겼다

046

Enough

Most parents have enough hope for their children

047

House

I want to look inside the house now

048

Friend

I want my friend to see me today

Most parents have enough hope for their children 대부분의 부모들은 그들의 아이들에 대해 충분한 희망을 가지고 있다 I want to look inside the house now 나는 지금 그 집 안을 보고 싶다 I want my friend to see me today 나는 오늘 내 친구가 나를 보았으면 좋겠다

049

In

What did he say in his last letter?

050

For

It is not important for you to know

051

Our

Our school is the best in the city

What did he say in his last letter? 그가 마지막 편지에서 뭐라고 말했니? **It is not important for you to know** 네가 아는 것은 중요하지 않다 **Our school is the best in the city** 우리 학교는 도시에서 최고다

052

mean

The king of this country is not mean

053

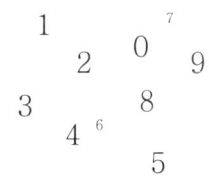

Number

Number seven is a good number in Korea

054

Different

Many people play different parts in their life

The king of this country is not mean 이 나라의 왕은 비열하지 않다 Number seven is a good number in Korea 숫자 7은 한국에서 좋은 숫자다 Many people play different parts in their life 사람들은 정말로 그들의 삶에서 다른 역할들을 맡는다

8words **133**

They kept on smiling even after she left 그들은 그녀가 떠나고 나서도 계속해서 미소를 지었다 **I will move out of his house soon** 나는 곧 그의 집에서 이사를 나갈 것이다 **That boy over there has a small face** 저기 저 소년은 작은 얼굴을 가졌다

Could you tell me the other love story? 내게 그 다른 사랑 이야기를 해줄래?
I really want to grow old with you 나는 정말로 너와 함께 나이를 먹고 싶다 I could not remember the other funny story 다른 재미있는 이야기가 기억나지않는다

061

Day

We started living near the sea that day

062

Mother

I know what your mother means to him

063

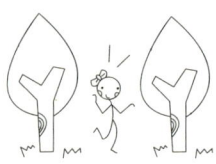

Between

I think it is between you and me

We started living near the sea that day 우리는 이날 바다 가까이에 살기 시작했다
I know what your mother means to him 나는 너의 어머니가 그에게 어떤 의미인지 안다
I think it is between you and me 나는 그것이 너와 나 사이의 일이라고 생각한다

064

Country

I want to live in a warm country

065

Leave

My best friend will never leave me again

066

Child

The child next to me has big eyes

I want to live in a warm country 나는 따뜻한 나라에 살기를 원한다 My best friend will never leave me again 나의 가장 친한 친구는 다시는 나를 떠나지 않을 것이다 The child next to me has big eyes 나의 옆의 아이는 커다란 눈을 가졌다

067

Group

The group of students waited for her today

068

Must

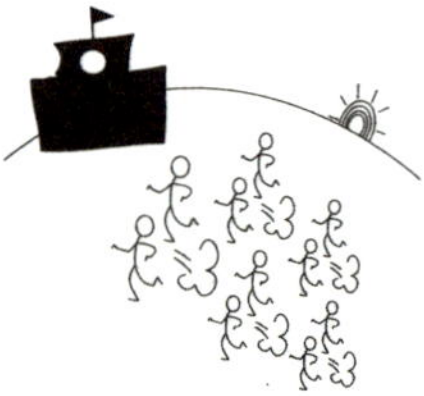

The big group of students must come today

069

He

He has known me for a long time

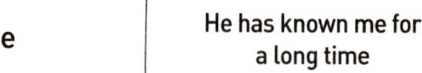

The group of students waited for her today 학생들의 무리가 오늘 그녀를 기다렸다
The big group of students must come today 학생들의 큰 무리가 오늘 와야 한다
He has known me for a long time 그는 나를 오랫동안 알아 왔다

070

Gone

My father will be gone for a day

071

Jogging

The old men are jogging in the park

072

Was

She was crying when her best friend called

My father will be gone for a day 나의 아버지는 하루 동안 안 계실 것이다 **The old men are jogging in the park** 그 노인들이 공원에서 조깅을 하고 있다 **She was crying when her best friend called** 그녀는 가장 친한 친구가 전화했을 때 울고 있었다

073
Helped

She helped her father bring the old table

074
Night

They often leave their old house at night

075
Time

I will see my friend some other time

She helped her father bring the old table 그녀는 아버지가 그 낡은 탁자를 가져오는 것을 도왔다 They often leave their old house at night 그들은 종종 밤에 옛 집을 떠났다 I will see my friend some other time 나는 또 언젠가 친구들을 만날 것이다

The morning sun is making me feel good 아침의 태양이 내 기분을 밝게 만들었다
I have nothing to say about your family 나는 너의 가족에 대해서 아무 것도 할말이 없다
She laughed so hard that she started crying 그녀는 너무 심하게 웃어서 울기 시작했다

This is why he has big black feet 이것이 그가 크고 검은 발을 가진 이유다 **He might have more money than the boy** 그가 소년보다 많은 돈을 가졌을 것이다 **The small, smiling little boy asked her out** 그 작고, 미소 짓는 어린 소년이 그녀에게 데이트를 신청했다

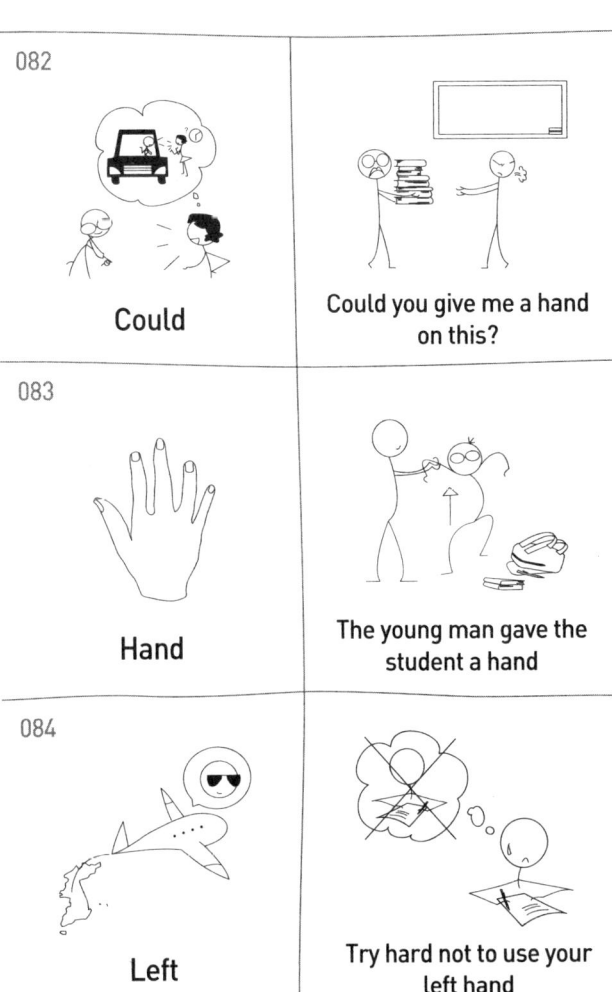

082 Could — Could you give me a hand on this?

083 Hand — The young man gave the student a hand

084 Left — Try hard not to use your left hand

Could you give me a hand on this? 이것 좀 도와줄 수 있니? The young man gave the student a hand 그 젊은 남자가 그 학생을 도왔다 Try hard not to use your left hand 왼손을 사용하지 않도록 최선을 다해라

085

School

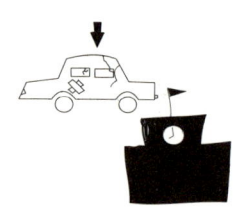

The car behind the school is very old

086

For

I want you to do something for me

087

Family

You must talk to your family about it

The car behind the school is very old 학교 뒤에 있는 그 차는 매우 오래되었다 **I want you to do something for me** 네가 나를 위해 무엇인가 해주기를 원한다 **You must talk to your family about it** 너는 가족에게 그것에 대해 말해야 한다

088
Am

I am your mother who gave you life

089
Leave

Our children want to leave the new city

090
Important

You have my name on that important paper

I am your mother who gave you life 나는 너에게 삶을 주었던 엄마이다
Our children want to leave the new city 우리 아이들은 새로운 도시로 떠나고 싶어한다 You have my name on that important paper 그 중요한 서류에 내 이름이 쓰여져 있다

091

Many

There are so many people jogging at night

092

But

He is not only kind but funny, too!

093

Blue

There is a blue ball under the table

There are so many people jogging at night 밤에 조깅하는 사람들이 매우 많다 **He is not only kind but funny, too!** 그는 친절할 뿐 아니라 재미있기도 하다 **There is a blue ball under the table** 탁자 밑에 파란색 공이 있다

094	
Paper	You have nothing to do with this paper
095	
Make	Could you make a sentence out of nothing?
096	
Parents	My parents will not let me go out

You have nothing to do with this paper 너는 이 서류와 관계가 없다 **Could you make a sentence out of nothing?** 너는 아무것도 없는 상태에서 문장을 만들 수 있니? **My parents will not let me go out** 나의 부모님이 못 나가게 할거야

097 Old — They saw the body in the old house

098 Every — Thank you for smiling at me every morning

099 Example — He just laughed after listening to my example

They saw the body in the old house 그들은 낡은 집에서 시체를 보았다　Thank you for smiling at me every morning 매일 아침 나에게 웃어줘서 고마워　He just laughed after listening to my example 그는 나의 예를 듣고 나서 그냥 웃었다

100	
Mean	Your parents are so mean to you today
101	
Them	I heard them say that my father died
102	
Call	It was really a close call for us!

Your parents are so mean to you today 너의 부모님은 오늘 너무 심술궂게 굴었다
I heard them say that my father died 그들이 나의 아버지가 돌아가셨다고 말하는 것을 들었다
It was really a close call for us! 우리 정말 위기 일발이었어!

103

Friend

He writes a letter to his other friend

104

Our

They are the best students in our school

105

Other

She is a teacher in the other school

He writes a letter to his other friend 그는 다른 친구에게 편지를 쓴다 **They are the best students in our school** 그들은 우리 학교 최고의 학생들이다 **She is a teacher in the other school** 그녀는 다른 학교의 교사다

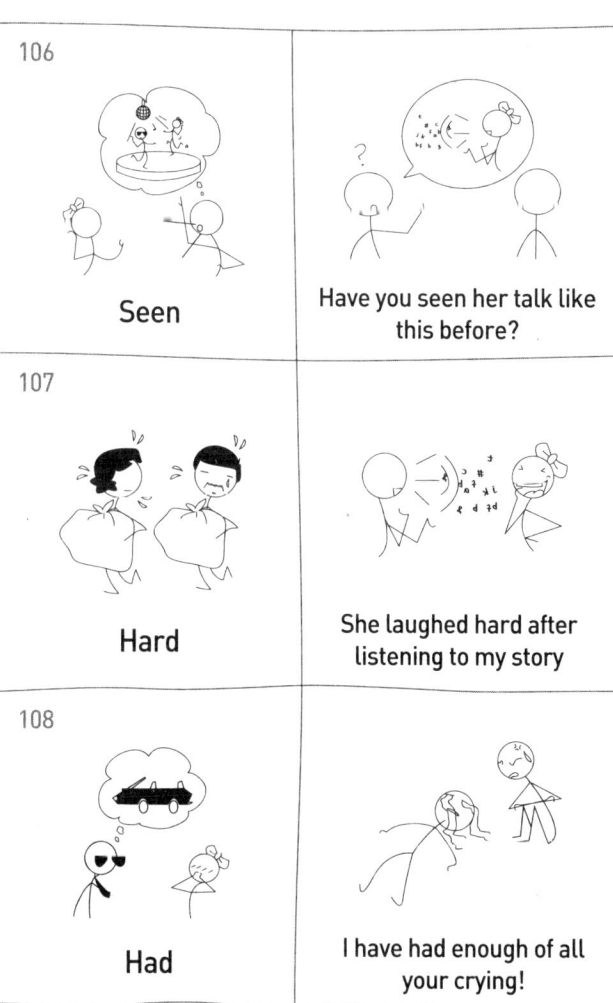

106	Seen	Have you seen her talk like this before?
107	Hard	She laughed hard after listening to my story
108	Had	I have had enough of all your crying!

Have you seen her talk like this before? 그녀가 전에 이렇게 말하는 걸 본 적이 있니?
She laughed hard after listening to my story 그녀는 나의 이야기를 듣고 나서 심하게 웃었다
I have had enough of all your crying! 너의 우는 소리는 이제 지긋지긋해

Do you want to make the first move? 네가 먼저 두고 싶니? **She asked me to look after her children** 그녀는 나에게 아이들을 돌봐달라고 부탁했다 **Name the most important part of your body** 너의 몸의 가장 중요한 부분을 말해봐라

We must take a rest before we go 우리 가기 전에 휴식을 좀 취해야 한다 I am ready to go with you now 나는 이제 너와 함께 갈 준비가 되었다 I love him more than my best friend 나는 그를 가장 친한 친구보다 더 사랑한다

8words **153**

115 Enough — Money is not enough to make her live

116 Room — There is a big table in her room

117 City — It is important to keep our city green

Money is not enough to make her live 돈은 그녀를 살게 하는 데 충분하지 않다 There is a big table in her room 그녀의 방에는 큰 탁자가 있다 It is important to keep our city green 우리의 도시를 녹색으로 유지하는 것은 중요하다

I think I have seen that play before 나는 저 연극을 전에 보았던 것 같다
I thought about your good idea last night 지난 밤 너의 아이디어에 대해 생각해 보았다
I think I have seen that man before 나는 저 남자를 전에 본 적이 있는 것 같다

121 Eyes — I saw them dancing before my very eyes

122 Make — You must make a letter for your parents

123 Car — I often see that car in the park

I saw them dancing before my very eyes 나는 그들이 춤추는 것을 바로 눈으로 봤다
You must make a letter for your parents 너는 부모님에게 편지를 써야 한다
I often see that car in the park 나는 저 자동차를 공원에서 자주 본다

124 Class — There are only a few students in class

125 Break — I saw him crying after your break up

126 Thing — Do they know how to use that thing?

There are only a few students in class 우리 반에는 아주 적은 수의 학생들밖에 없다 I saw him crying after your break up 나는 너희들이 헤어진 후에 그가 울고 있는 것을 보았다 Do they know how to use that thing? 그들은 저 물건을 어떻게 사용하는지 아니?

127
Dancing

I see her dancing most of the time

128
Name

Name the most important parts of this car

129
Her

The child is crying to her teacher now

I see her dancing most of the time 나는 주로 그녀가 춤추는 것을 본다 **Name the most important parts of this car** 이 자동차의 가장 중요한 부품들의 이름을 대라 **The child is crying to her teacher now** 그 아이는 지금 선생님에게 울며 애원하고 있다

130

Several

There were several parents in our school today

131

Cold

He was a little cold to me today

132

Time

Do you still have time for your family?

There were several parents in our school today 오늘 우리 학교에 몇몇 부모들이 있다
He was a little cold to me today 그는 오늘 내게 약간 쌀쌀맞았다 Do you still have time for your family? 너에게 아직 가족들을 위한 시간이 있니?

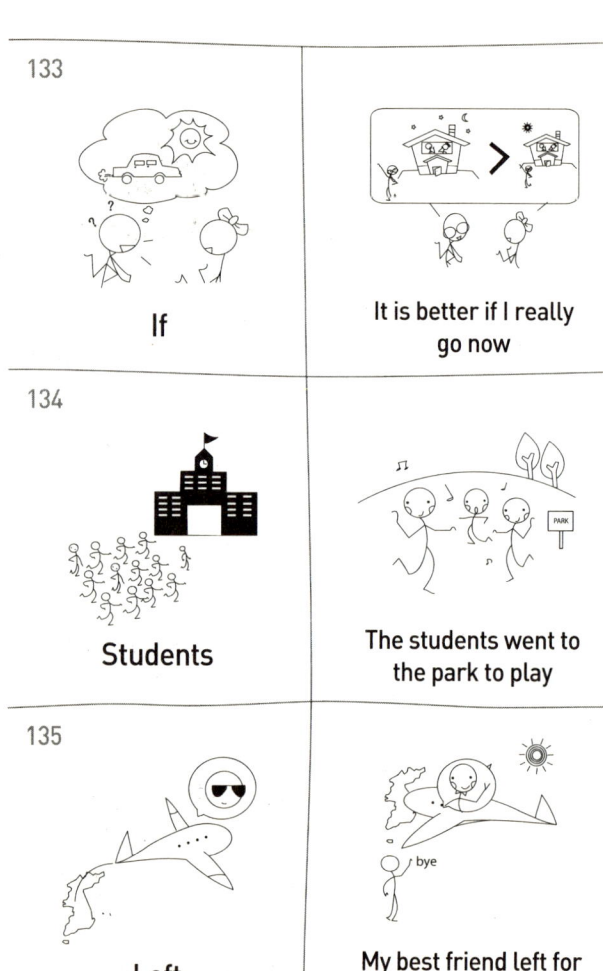

It is better if I really go now 내가 지금 정말로 간다면 더 낫다 The students went to the park to play 그 학생들은 공원에 놀러 갔다 My best friend left for Korea this morning 나의 가장 친한 친구가 오늘 아침 한국으로 떠났다

Say thank you to your parents for me 내 대신 너의 부모님께 고맙다고 말씀 드려
I have to hand in my paper today 나는 오늘 내 서류를 제출해야 한다   **I found a small fly in my food** 나는 내 음식에서 작은 파리를 발견했다

139
Live

My friend will live in Korea for good

140
Have

You have to do something very important today

141
Held

The ball was held in the new room

My friend will live in Korea for good 나의 친구는 한국에서 계속 살 것이다
You have to do something very important today 나는 오늘 무엇인가 아주 중요한 일을 해야 한다   **The ball was held in the new room** 무도회는 새로운 방에서 열렸다

142

We

We waited for the students in the room

143

Than

I want to be better than the rest

144

Warm

The food on the table is still warm

We waited for the students in the room 우리는 그 방에서 학생들을 기다렸다
I want to be better than the rest 나는 나머지보다 더 낫기를 원한다   The food on the table is still warm 탁자 위의 음식은 아직 따뜻하다

145
Early

I left the house early in the morning

146
City

My parents will go to the city today

147
Great

I have a great idea for the play

I left the house early in the morning 나는 아침 일찍 그 집을 떠났다 **My parents will go to the city today** 나의 부모님은 오늘 그 도시에 가셨다 **I have a great idea for the play** 나에게 그 연극에 대한 멋진 아이디어가 있다

148

Who

Who will go with you to the city?

149

Korea

It was very cold in Korea last night

150

Rest

You may have the rest of the money

Who will go with you to the city? 누가 너와 함께 그 도시에 가니? It was very cold in Korea last night 지난 밤 한국은 매우 추웠다 You may have the rest of the money 네가 나머지 돈을 가져도 좋다

151

Together

We have to look at the house together

152

Has

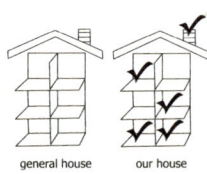

Our house has more than five different parts

153

Was

He was my best friend in high school

We have to look at the house together 우리는 오늘 그 집을 봐야 한다
Our house has more than five different parts 우리 집에는 다섯 개 이상의 다른 부분이 있다 **He was my best friend in high school** 그는 고등학교 때 나의 가장 친한 친구였다

We were told to stop the show today 우리는 오늘 쇼를 그만두라는 말을 들었다
They must have new children for the show 그들은 쇼를 위해 새로운 아이들을 구해야 한다 **The best life is living it with love** 최고의 삶은 사랑과 함께 살아가는 것이다

157

children

There were three children behind the green car

158

Green

I saw three children behind the green car

159

Table

There is a big table in my room

There were three children behind the green car 녹색 자동차 뒤에 세 명의 아이들이 있었다 **I saw three children behind the green car** 나는 녹색 차 뒤에서 세 명의 아이들을 보았다 **There is a big table in my room** 내 방에는 커다란 탁자가 있다

160

Class

The rest of the class started to leave

161

Warm

I waited for the food to get warm

162

Black

The big black car she saw was his

The rest of the class started to leave 학급의 나머지가 떠나기 시작했다   I waited for the food to get warm 나는 음식이 따뜻해지기를 기다렸다   The big black car she saw was his 그녀가 본 커다란 검은색 차는 그의 것이었다

163

Among

Among my students came just one good answer

164

You

I know she will do good without you

165

Like

I do not like to be left behind

Among my students came just one good answer 나의 학생들 가운데서 단지 한 가지 훌륭한 답만이 나왔다 **I know she will do good without you** 나는 그녀가 너 없이도 잘해낼 것을 안다 **I do not like to be left behind** 나는 뒤에 남겨지는 것을 좋아하지 않는다

We will be very good students in class 우리는 학급에서 아주 뛰어난 학생이 될 것이다 **I did not see my intelligent teacher today** 나는 오늘 지적인 선생님을 보지 못했다 **My parents will be back from Korea soon** 나의 부모님이 곧 한국에서 돌아오실 것이다

169

Light

The light from her room could be seen

170

Different

She started attending a different class this morning

171

Move

I did nothing to make her move out

The light from her room could be seen 그녀의 방에서 나오는 빛을 볼 수 있었다
She started attending a different class this morning 그녀는 오늘 아침 다른 수업을 듣기 시작했다 I did nothing to make her move out 나는 그녀가 이사가게 만들만한 아무 짓도 하지 않았다

172

Since

I have seen her crying since you left

173

Could

She left so she could take a rest

174

Nine

There are nine students living in the house

I have seen her crying since you left 나는 네가 떠난 이래로 그녀가 우는 것을 보고있다 She left so she could take a rest 그녀는 휴식을 취하러 떠났다 There are nine students living in the house 이 집에 아홉 명의 학생들이 살고 있다

I have heard the same story from him 나는 그로부터 같은 이야기를 들었다
The intelligent child did great in the show 그 총명한 아이는 쇼에서 훌륭히 해냈다
Did you find the ball behind his back? 그의 등 뒤에서 그 공을 찾았니?

178

Only

Parents only want the best for their children

179

Died

My parents died when I was a child

180

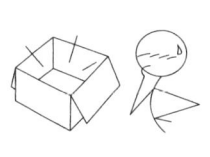

Nothing

Nothing can stop her from living with him

Parents only want the best for their children 부모들은 오직 그들의 아이들을 위해 가장 좋은 것을 원한다 My parents died when I was a child 나의 부모님은 내가 어렸을 때 돌아가셨다 Nothing can stop her from living with him 아무 것도 그녀가 그와 함께 사는 것을 막을 수 없었다

I saw it on top of the tree 나는 그것을 나무 꼭대기에서 보았다 **The big fire made us leave the house** 큰 화재가 우리를 그 집에서 떠나게 만들었다 **I had a great time with my friend** 나는 친구와 멋진 시간을 보냈다

184

Your

I want to talk to your mother today

185

Can

Can I see you today after your class?

186

Who

Who do you think you are to me?

I want to talk to your mother today 나는 오늘 너의 어머니와 이야기하기를 원한다   Can I see you today after your class? 오늘 수업 끝나고 너를 만날 수 있니?
Who do you think you are to me? 너는 내가 어떤 사람이라고 생각해?

She is smiling but she is crying inside 그녀는 웃고 있지만 속으로는 울고 있다
I have never seen him do something good 나는 그가 무엇인가 좋은 일을 하는 것을 본 적이 없다 **My students bring out the best in me** 나의 학생들은 내가 최상의 능력을 발휘하게 만든다

Something started to move in the blue room 무엇인가 그 파란 방에서 움직이기 시작했다 **My friend gave me a ride to school** 나의 친구가 학교에 태워다 주었다
I am sure I never saw him before 나는 그를 전에 본 적이 없다고 확신한다

193 Both

I helped both children but they still died

194 Him

How do you show your love for him?

195 Move

We must move to the next room now

I helped both children but they still died 나는 두 아이를 모두 도왔지만 그래도 그들은 죽었다 **How do you show your love for him?** 너는 어떻게 그에 대한 너의 사랑을 보여주니? **We must move to the next room now** 우린 지금 옆방으로 가야 한다

196
Some

I saw some students jogging in the park

197
The

The mean man is inside the big house

198
Of

They will move out of the house today

I saw some students jogging in the park 나는 몇몇 학생들이 공원에서 조깅하는 것을 보았다 The mean man is inside the big house 그 비열한 남자는 그 커다란 집 안에 있다 They will move out of the house today 그들은 오늘 그 집에서 이사 나갈 것이다

199 **On**

Why do you keep on smiling at her?

200 **Table**

Let us go to the table and eat

201 **Last**

I saw the three of you last night

Why do you keep on smiling at her? 왜 너는 계속 그녀에게 미소 짓니? **Let us go to the table and eat** 식탁으로 가서 먹자 **I saw the three of you last night** 나는 어젯밤 너희 셋을 보았다

202

Early

They leave their new house early every morning

203

Morning

They only go to school in the morning

204

Keep

My father asked me to keep his money

They leave their new house early every morning 그들은 매일 아침 일찍 새 집을 나선다 **They only go to school in the morning** 그들은 아침에만 학교에 간다
My father asked me to keep his money 나의 아버지가 그의 돈을 보관해 달라고 부탁했다

8words

205

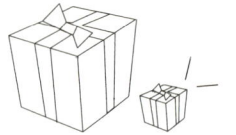

Small

She must love dancing in that small park

206

Front

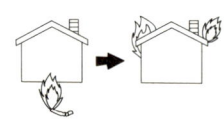

The fire started in front of the house

207

Thought

I never thought that you could do that

She must love dancing in that small park 그녀는 작은 공원에서 춤추기를 좋아하는 것이 틀림없다   The fire started in front of the house 화재는 그 집 앞쪽에서 시작되었다   I never thought that you could do that 나는 네가 그걸 해낼 수 있을 거라고 생각해본 적이 없었다

It took him some time to think over 그가 생각하는 데 좀 시간이 걸렸다 I had cold feet when I saw him 나는 그를 보고 도망칠 자세를 취했다 I have a big table in my room 나는 방에 큰 탁자를 가지고 있다

211

Making

You can never stop me from making money

212

Does

It does not make you a good mother

213

From

The little boy from Korea can jump high

You can never stop me from making money 너는 내가 돈 버는 것을 절대 막을 수 없다 **It does not make you a good mother** 그것은 너를 좋은 엄마로 만들어주지 않는다 **The little boy from Korea can jump high** 한국에서 온 그 어린 소년은 높이 뛸 수 있다

214

Enough

I have enough time to talk with you

215

car

The body of his car is not great

216

With

Will you go to school with us today?

I have enough time to talk with you 나는 너와 이야기할 충분한 시간이 있다
The body of his car is not great 그의 자동차의 몸체는 훌륭하지 않다 Will you go to school with us today? 오늘 우리와 같이 학교에 갈래?

217

They

Do you think they can live without us?

218

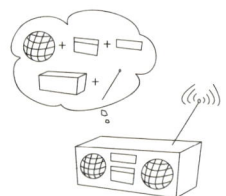

Parts

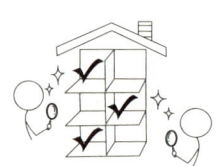

Let us learn the parts of the house

219

Learn

Students learn the different parts of the car

Do you think they can live without us? 그들이 우리 없이 살 수 있다고 생각해?
Let us learn the parts of the house 집의 부분들에 대해서 공부하자 **Students learn the different parts of the car** 학생들은 차의 여러 가지 부분들을 배웠다

220

Read

My mother read your love letter for me

221

Most

Most of us wish for a great life

222

Until

I still live with my parents until now

My mother read your love letter for me 나의 어머니가 위해 너의 연애 편지를 읽어주었다 Most of us wish for a great life 우리 중 대부분은 훌륭한 삶을 바란다
I still live with my parents until now 나는 지금까지 여전히 부모님과 함께 살고 있다

223

For

Korea is really a great country for her

224

Night

The man waited for the boy last night

225

Ball

The big black ball is in the house

Korea is really a great country for her 한국은 그녀에게 정말 멋진 나라다
The man waited for the boy last night 그 남자는 지난 밤 그 소년을 기다렸다 **The big black ball is in the house** 그 커다랗고 검은 공이 집 안에 있다

226

Like

They said they like jogging at the park

227

Too

My family will live in the city, too

228

Try

People will try to talk about it soon

They said they like jogging at the park 그들은 공원에서 조깅하는 것을 좋아한다고 말했다 **My family will live in the city, too** 나의 가족도 그 도시에서 살 것이다 **People will try to talk about it soon** 사람들은 곧 그것에 대해 이야기하려고 시도할 것이다

229

Told

She told me she said yes to Youngchoon

230

Every

She writes to her best friend every day

231

Face

Do you remember the face of that boy?

She told me she said yes to Youngchoon 그녀는 영춘에게 승낙했다고 나에게 말했다 **She writes to her best friend every day** 그녀는 가장 친한 친구에게 매일 편지를 쓴다 **Do you remember the face of that boy?** 너는 그 아이의 얼굴이 기억나니?

232

Most

You must make the most out of it

233

what

What is your part in the school play?

234

Part

I do not want to part with him

You must make the most out of it 너는 그것을 최대한 이용해야 한다 What is your part in the school play? 그 학교 연극에서 너의 역할은 뭐니? I do not want to part with him 나는 그와 헤어지는 것을 원하지 않는다

I will only say 'yes' to this man 나는 이 남자에게 '예스'라고만 말할 것이다
He helped his teacher in making the story 그는 선생님이 그 이야기를 짓는 것을 도왔다   I do not want to go home early 나는 오늘 집에 일찍 가고 싶지 않다

238

Did

I did not use my car this morning

239

Children

The children will be attending an important class

240

Story

The story my mother told me was funny

I did not use my car this morning 나는 오늘 아침 나의 차를 사용하지 않았다
The children will be attending an important class 그 아이들은 중요한 수업에 참여할 것이다　The story my mother told me was funny 나의 어머니가 들려준 이야기는 재미있었다

241

Am

I am making a letter for my teacher

242

Also

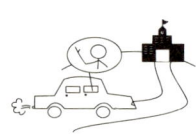

Do you also take your car to school?

243

Use

My parents let me use the family car

I am making a letter for my teacher 나는 선생님께 편지를 쓰고 있다 **Do you also take your car to school?** 너도 자동차를 타고 학교에 가니? **My parents let me use the family car** 나의 부모님이 가족 자동차를 쓰도록 해주셨다

244

Next

We have to wait for the next class

245

Were

I thought there were students in the school

246

Come

Let us wait for the teacher to come

We have to wait for the next class 우리는 다음 수업을 기다려야 한다   I thought there were students in the school 학생들이 학교 안에 있는 것 같았다   Let us wait for the teacher to come 선생님이 오시기를 기다리자

Your example is not enough for the students 너의 예는 학생들에게 충분하지 않다
It is hard to live in the city 도시 안에서 사는 것은 힘들다   **Do we really have to wait for her?** 우리가 정말 그녀를 기다려야 해?

I could not wait to see my mother 어머니를 빨리 보고 싶어서 참을 수가 없었다
The teacher spoke in front of the students 선생님이 학생들 앞에서 말했다   I will call him in about an hour 약 한 시간 내로 그에게 전화할 것이다

B Words
Review

영춘선생이 일러주는 Review 활용법!

1. 그림과 문장을 보고 의미를 파악합니다
되도록이면 해석을 보지 않고 영어 그대로의
의미를 파악하도록 노력하세요!

2. MP3로 Review 부분을 들으면서 네이티브들의 정확한 발음을 청취합니다
네이티브들의 문장은 두 번씩 반복 됩니다.
처음에는 발음을 청취를 하고 두 번째는 조용히 따라 읽습니다.

3. 이제 Review 부분을 큰 소리 내어 읽습니다
영어는 마음속에 담아두기 위해 배우는 언어가 아닙니다.
마음껏 소리치면서 읽으세요!
단, 전철이나 버스 같은 대중교통에서 책을 읽으시는 분들은
주위 사람들에게 피해가 가지 않게 특별히 조심해 주세요!

★주로 대중교통을 이용하는 영춘선생이 이 책을 들고 다니시는 분을 뵙게 되면
친필 싸인을 즉시 제공하겠습니다.

Review

→ 001

I called her but she did not answer

223 ←

Korea is really a great country for her

→ 003

I love jogging with my students every morning

213 ←

The little boy from Korea can jump high

→ 013

Say "Thank you" to those who helped you

194 ←

How do you show your love for him?

She writes to her best friend every day

I had cold feet when I saw him

He helped his teacher in making the story

My father asked me to keep his money

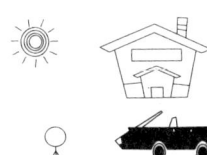

I did not use my car this morning

I saw some students jogging in the park

→ 020

Their house is not very far from here

188 ←

I have never seen him do something good

→ 025

I think I heard her crying last night

175 ←

I have heard the same story from him

→ 033

Is she the first or the second child?

170 ←

She started attending a different class this morning

My parents let me use the family car

We will be very good students in class

We have to wait for the next class

My parents will be back from Korea soon

Let us wait for the teacher to come

I have seen her crying since you left

→ 038

There was a big fire in the city

165 ←

I do not like to be left behind

→ 045

He just left a letter on the table

153 ←

He was my best friend in high school

→ 051

Our school is the best in the city

110 ←

She asked me to look after her children

It is hard to live
in the city

Parents only want the best
for their children

The teacher spoke in front
of the students

I want to talk to your
mother today

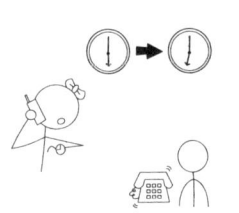

I will call him in about
an hour

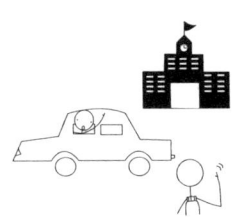

My friend gave me a
ride to school

→ 056

I will move out of his house soon

115 ←

Money is not enough to make her live

→ 063

I think it is between you and me

116 ←

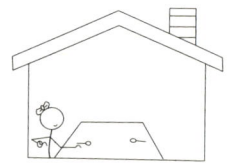

There is a big table in her room

→ 067

The group of students waited for her today

105 ←

She is a teacher in the other school

→ 233 | 138 ←

What is your part in the school play? | I found a small fly in my food

→ 227 | 113 ←

My family will live in the city, too | I am ready to go with you now

→ 222 | 125 ←

I still live with my parents until now | I saw him crying after your break up

→ 069

He has known me for a long time

104 ←

They are the best students in our school

→ 075

I will see my friend some other time

093 ←

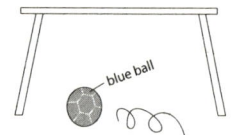

There is a blue ball under the table

→ 086

I want you to do something for me

087 ←

You must talk to your family about it

→ 216

Will you go to school with us today?

131 ←

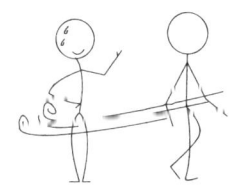

He was a little cold to me today

→ 215

The body of his car is not great

126 ←

Do they know how to use that thing?

→ 214

I have enough time to talk with you

143 ←

I want to be better than the rest

Speaking English

using **9 Words**

"9단어로 영어를 말할 수 있어요!"

목표가 있는 자는
이 책이 손에서 떠나지 않는다
_영춘선생

 **9 Words**

001

| An | An old friend was on the morning paper today |

002

| Since | I have known him since I was a child |

003

| House | Their house was right next to our old house |

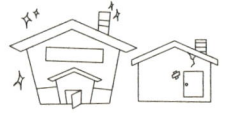

An old friend was on the morning paper today 옛 친구가 오늘 아침 신문에 나왔다
I have known him since I was a child 나는 그를 어렸을 때부터 알아왔다 **Their house was right next to our old house** 그들의 집은 그 우리의 옛집 바로 옆에 있었다

004

City

I saw an old friend living in the city

005

Wished

I thought that he wished to speak to me

006

Paper

The morning paper was on the table early today

I saw an old friend living in the city 나는 그 도시에서 살고 있는 옛 친구를 보았다
I thought that he wished to speak to me 나는 그가 나에게 말을 걸기를 원했다고 생각했다 The morning paper was on the table early today 오늘 일찍 아침 신문이 탁자 위에 있었다

007

same

We went to the same school in the city

008

Remember

I remember jogging to school with him every morning

009

Both

He left when both his mother and father died

We went to the same school in the city 우리는 그 도시에서 같은 학교에 다녔다
I remember jogging to school with him every morning 나는 그와 함께 매일 아침 학교까지 조깅했던 것을 기억한다 **He left when both his mother and father died** 그는 어머니와 아버지가 두 분 다 돌아가셨을 때 떠났다

010
Parts
Most parts must be kept inside the small room

011
Sun
I saw her smiling at the sun this morning

012
Green
The new green car next to me is his

Most parts must be kept inside the small room 대부분의 부품들은 그 작은 방 안에 보관해야 한다 I saw her smiling at the sun this morning 나는 오늘 아침 그녀가 태양을 향해 미소 짓는 것을 보았다 The new green car next to me is his 나의 옆에 있는 그 새로운 녹색 자동차는 그의 것이다

013

Went

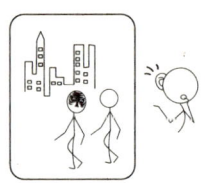

I heard he went to the city with Youngchoon

014

Attending

They started attending a dancing school for young people

015

Best

They are now the best at dancing in Korea

I heard he went to the city with Youngchoon 나는 그가 영춘과 함께 그 도시로 갔다고 들었다 **They started attending a dancing school for young people** 그들은 젊은 사람들을 위한 댄스 학교에 다니기 시작했다 **They are now the best at dancing in Korea** 그들은 이제 한국에서 가장 춤을 잘 춘다

016

Food

We love to find good food on the table

017

Ready

I am not ready to go with you now

018

Hour

It took him an hour to eat the food

We love to find good food on the table 우리는 식탁 위에서 좋은 음식을 찾는 것을 즐긴다 **I am not ready to go with you now** 나는 지금 너와 함께 갈 준비가 되지 않았다 **It took him an hour to eat the food** 그가 그 음식을 먹는데 한 시간이 걸렸다

019 **Top** — I will go to school in my green top

020 **Very** — He is a very good example to the children

021 **Country** — I love my family and my country very much

I will go to school in my green top 나는 녹색 상의를 입고 학교에 갈 것이다   He is a very good example to the children 그는 아이들에게 매우 좋은 예다   I love my family and my country very much 나는 가족과 나라를 무척 사랑한다

022

Smiling

She was smiling at me when I left home

023

Wished

My three little children wished something great for me

024

Helped

Several people knew he helped them out in this

She was smiling at me when I left home 그녀는 내가 집을 나설 때 내게 미소 지었다
My three little children wished something great for me 나의 세 명의 아이들은 나를 위해 뭔가 대단한 것을 빌었다 **Several people knew he helped them out in this** 몇몇 사람들은 그가 그들을 이것으로부터 구출했다는 것을 알았다

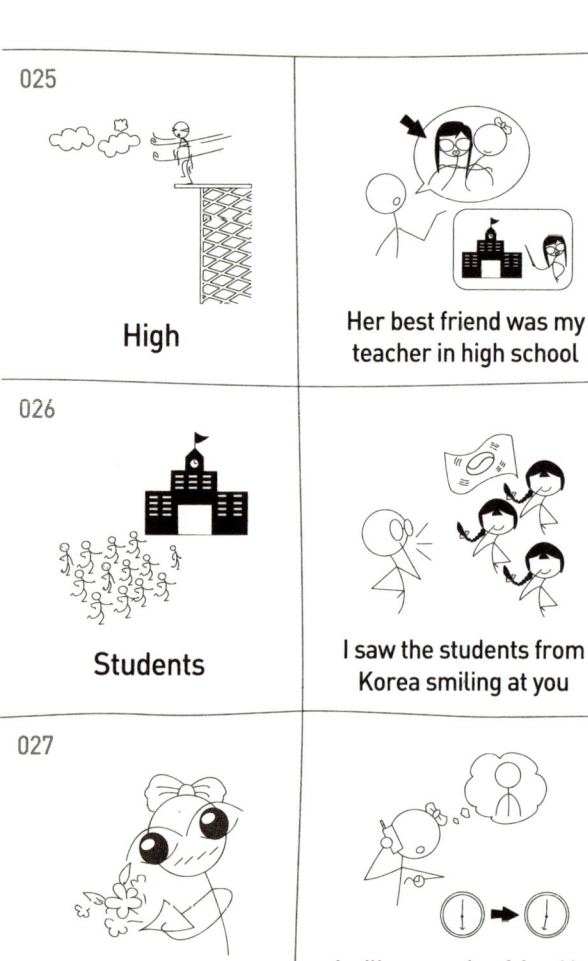

025 **High** — Her best friend was my teacher in high school

026 **Students** — I saw the students from Korea smiling at you

027 **See** — I will see my boyfriend in about an hour

Her best friend was my teacher in high school 그녀의 가장 친한 친구가 고등학교 때 나의 선생님이었다 **I saw the students from Korea smiling at you** 나는 한국에서 온 학생들이 너에게 미소 짓는 것을 보았다 **I will see my boyfriend in about an hour** 나는 한 시간내로 나의 남자친구를 만날 것이다

028

Boy

Your boy waited for you here until early morning

029

Writes

She writes a letter for her child in Korea

030

Means

I know what your mother means to the people

Your boy waited for you here until early morning 너의 아들이 이른 아침까지 여기서 너를 기다렸다 **She writes a letter for her child in Korea** 그녀는 한국에 있는 아이에게 편지를 쓴다 **I know what your mother means to the people** 나는 너의 어머니가 사람들에게 어떤 의미인지 안다

9words

031

Boy

That boy can run
as fast as a car

032

Little

The little boy is smiling
at the old man

033

You

Dancing and jogging are
good for you and me

That boy can run as fast as a car 그 소년은 자동차만큼 빨리 달릴 수 있다 **The little boy is smiling at the old man** 그 어린 소년은 그 노인에게 미소 짓고 있다 **Dancing and jogging are good for you and me** 춤과 조깅은 너와 나에게 유익하다

034

Laughed

I know why your mother laughed at that child

035

Them

I know why his family must go with them

036

Between

I think there is something between you and him

I know why your mother laughed at that child 나는 왜 너의 어머니가 그 아이를 비웃었는지 안다 I know why his family must go with them 나는 왜 그의 가족이 그들과 함께 가야 하는지 안다 I think there is something between you and him 나는 너와 그 사이에 무엇인가 있다고 생각한다

037

Your

I want to go to your house after school

038

Park

I want to see him jogging at the park

039

Think

I think this is not enough for my children

I want to go to your house after school 나는 학교가 끝나고 너의 집에 가기를 원한다 **I want to see him jogging at the park** 나는 그가 공원에서 조깅하는 것을 보고 싶다
I think this is not enough for my children 나는 이것이 나의 아이들에게 충분하지 않다고 생각한다

040

In

I know why they waited for her in school

041

Must

The big group of students must come early today

042

Kind

The father and mother of that family are kind

I know why they waited for her in school 나는 왜 그들이 학교에서 그녀를 기다렸는지 안다
The big group of students must come early today 학생들의 큰 무리가 반드시 오늘 일찍 와야 한다 The father and mother of that family are kind 그 가족의 아버지와 어머니는 친절하다

043	
Never	She never meant to make love with the king
044	
Seven	A group of seven people told them to wait
045	
Intelligent	I am listening to the group of intelligent students

She never meant to make love with the king 그녀는 왕과 사랑을 나눌 뜻이 전혀 없었다
A group of seven people told them to wait 일곱 명의 무리가 그들에게 기다리라고 말했다
I am listening to the group of intelligent students 나는 총명한 학생들의 무리에서 귀를 기울이고 있다

046

School

Have you heard about the little boy in school?

047

Knew

He knew me when I was still a boy

048

Each

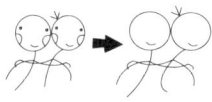

They have known each other since they were children

Have you heard about the little boy in school? 학교에서 그 작은 소년에 대해 들어봤니? He knew me when I was still a boy 내가 소년일 때 그는 나를 알았다 They have known each other since they were children 그들은 아이 때부터 서로를 알아왔다

049

Talked

She has talked about Youngchoon for a long time

050

Great

It was great to have seen his face again

051

Meant

I never meant to find out about it first

She has talked about Youngchoon for a long time 그녀는 영춘에 대해 오랫동안 이야기해 왔다 **It was great to have seen his face again** 그의 얼굴을 다시 봐서 좋았다 **I never meant to find out about it first** 나는 그것에 대해 처음으로 알아낼 의도가 없었다

It is important to think first before you speak 네가 말하기 전에 먼저 생각하는 것이 중요하다 I can feel some students are listening to us 나는 몇몇 학생들이 우리에게 귀를 기울이는 것을 느낄수 있다 I thought you were the right man for me 나는 네가 나에게 맞는 사람이라고 생각했다

055 Later — I will go to school with my mother later

056 Ready — Are you ready to make a letter for him?

057 Now — Are you now ready to make a small fire?

I will go to school with my mother later 나는 나중에 어머니와 함께 학교에 갈 것이다 Are you ready to make a letter for him? 그에게 편지를 쓸 준비가 되었니? Are you now ready to make a small fire? 이제 작은 불을 피울 준비가 되었니?

The people in that city died because of fire 그 도시의 사람들은 화재 때문에 죽었다
The story that the teacher told was very funny 선생님이 해준 이야기는 아주 재미있었다
She might go with them without the black car 그녀는 그 검은색 자동차 없이 그들과 함께 갈 수도 있다

My friend and I had a great time last night 나의 친구와 나는 지난 밤 멋진 시간을 보냈다 **I did not have enough money to go out** 나는 외출할 만큼 충분한 돈이 없었다 **What is the most important part of your face?** 너의 얼굴에서 가장 중요한 부분이 무엇이니?

064

To

Her dancing is a good example to the children

065

Day

They have to close the park for one day

066

Morning

This morning my parents left the house for jogging

Her dancing is a good example to the children 그녀의 춤은 아이들에게 좋은 본보기다
They have to close the park for one day 그들은 하루 동안 공원을 닫아야 한다
This morning my parents left the house for jogging 오늘 아침 나의 부모님이 조깅을 하려고 집을 나섰다

How do you show your love to your parents? 너는 부모님께 네 사랑을 어떻게 보여드리니?
You may never see the friend you once knew 너는 네가 한때 알았던 친구를 다시는 못 볼 수도 있다
You mean so much to the high school students 너는 그 고등학교 학생들에게 매우 큰 의미가 있다

I wanted to talk to you about the children 나는 너와 아이들에 대해 이야기하고 싶었다 **Why do you have to leave her so soon?** 왜 너는 그렇게 빨리 그녀를 떠나야 하니?
I wanted to talk to you about the play 나는 너와 연극에 대해 이야기하고 싶었다

073

Few

Only a few men could be great parents today

074

Got

I got a new green house from my love

075

Started

Once you started out, you can never go back

Only a few men could be great parents today 오늘날에는 아주 적은 수의 사람들만이 훌륭한 부모가 될 수 있다 I got a new green house from my love 나는 나의 연인에게서 새로운 녹색 집을 받았다 Once you started out, you can never go back 일단 떠나면 다시는 돌아갈 수 없다

076

Park

I live in a small house near the park

077

Small

My father has a small house in the country

078

Money

I want to give him half of my money

I live in a small house near the park 나는 공원 가까이에 있는 작은 집에 산다
My father has a small house in the country 나의 아버지는 시골에 작은 집을 가지고 있다 I want to give him half of my money 나는 그에게 내 돈의 절반을 주고 싶다

9words

079
Find

Give me enough time to find a new teacher

080
Many

Many young students keep jogging with the big group

081
Known

I have never known a great man like you

Give me enough time to find a new teacher 나에게 새로운 교사를 찾을 충분한 시간을 다오
Many young students keep jogging with the big group 많은 어린 학생들이 그 큰 무리에서 조깅을 계속한다 **I have never known a great man like you** 나는 한 번도 너처럼 훌륭한 사람을 알았던 적이 없다

082

Sure

I am sure he will come back to me

083

Table

I want to get a table for my room

084

Called

He was in the car when I called him

I am sure he will come back to me 나는 그가 나에게 돌아올 것이라고 확신한다
I want to get a table for my room 나는 내 방에 놓을 탁자를 갖고 싶다 He was in the car when I called him 내가 그를 불렀을 때 그는 차 안에 있었다

085
Know

You did not let me know from the start

086
Look

Your eyes are smiling when you look at me

087
Close

No one died but it was a close call!

You did not let me know from the start 너는 내에게 처음부터 알려주지 않았다 Your eyes are smiling when you look at me 니가 나를 볼 때면 네 눈은 웃고 있다 No one died but it was a close call! 아무도 죽지 않았지만 구사 일생이었다!

088

Sea

I want to go to the sea with him

089

Rest

I could not remember the rest of the show

090

Food

There was no more food when I got home

I want to go to the sea with him 나는 그와 함께 바다에 가고 싶다 I could not remember the rest of the show 나는 쇼의 나머지를 기억하지 못했다 There was no more food when I got home 내가 집에 왔을 때는 더 이상 음식이 없었다

9words **243**

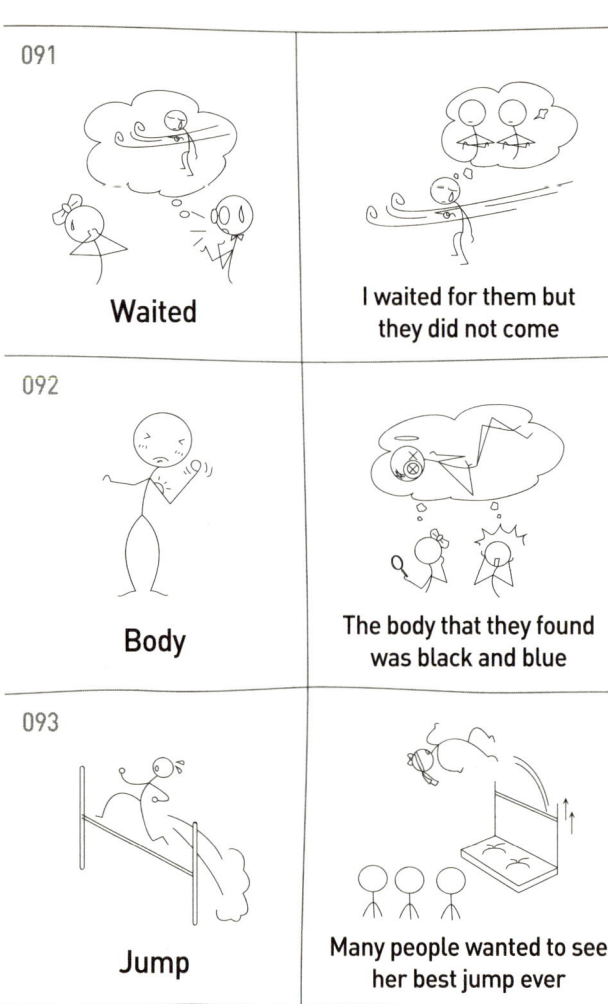

091 Waited
I waited for them but they did not come

092 Body
The body that they found was black and blue

093 Jump
Many people wanted to see her best jump ever

I waited for them but they did not come 나는 그들을 기다렸지만 그들은 오지 않았다
The body that they found was black and blue 그들이 찾아낸 시체는 검고 푸른색이었다(시퍼렇게 멍이 들어 있었다) Many people wanted to see her best jump ever 많은 사람들이 그녀의 훌륭한 점프를 보고 싶어했다

My father told my mother about the school ball 나의 아버지는 내 어머니에게 학교 무도회에 대해 이야기했다 **My mother asked me to bring some brown paper** 나의 어머니는 내게 갈색 포장지를 좀 가져오라고 시켰다 **He must have gone out with his best friend** 그는 가장 친한 친구와 놀러 간 것이 틀림없다

I have nothing if I do not have you 나는 널 가지지 못하면 가진 게 아무 것도 없다
It is very important that you call her today 네가 오늘 그녀에게 전화하는 것이 아주 중요하다
The children saw the face of the old man 그 아이들은 그 노인의 얼굴을 보았다

Do I look like my mother or my father? 내가 어머니를 닮았어 아니면 아버지를 닮았어? I was still up at three in the morning 나는 새벽 세 시에도 여전히 깨어 있었다 Do you think we could still eat that food? 너는 우리가 아직 저 음식을 먹을 수 있다고 생각하니?

103

Soon

Her only wish is to be with him soon

104

Really

Are you really ready to go back to school?

105

Often

My parents often give money to the old man

Her only wish is to be with him soon 그녀의 유일한 소원은 빨리 그와 함께있는 것이다
Are you really ready to go back to school? 너는 정말로 학교에 돌아갈 준비가 되었니?
My parents often give money to the old man 나의 부모님은 종종 그 노인에게 돈을 준다

106 Us
The children asked us to bring the new car

107 Number
Give me your number so I can call you

108 Sentence
My teacher asked me to read the first sentence

The children asked us to bring the new car 그 아이들은 우리에게 새 차를 가져오라고 요청했다 Give me your number so I can call you 내가 전화할 수 있게 너의 전화번호를 다오 My teacher asked me to read the first sentence 나의 선생님이 나에게 첫 문장을 읽으라고 시켰다

109

School

I saw your boy with those children in school

110

Means

This means we have to go to school early

111

Short

My teacher asked me to read the short story

I saw your boy with those children in school 나는 학교에서 당신 아이가 그 아이들과 함께 있는 것을 보았다 **This means we have to go to school early** 이것은 우리가 학교에 일찍 가야 한다는 것을 뜻한다 **My teacher asked me to read the short story** 나의 선생님이 내게 그 짧은 이야기를 읽으라고 시켰다

112

Attending

He talked about the boy attending the same class

113

Such

The teacher inside the car talked without such class

114

Black

The man in the black car asked her out

He talked about the boy attending the same class 그는 같은 수업에 참여하는 아이에 관하여 이야기 했다 The teacher inside the car talked without such class 자동차 안에 있었던 그 교사는 너무나 품위없이 말했다 The man in the black car asked her out 검은색 차에 탄 그 남자가 그녀에게 데이트를 신청했다

115

Cold

It is still very cold in my room today

116

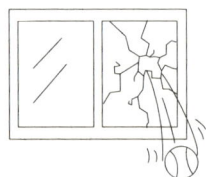

Break

Do we really have to break up, my love?

117

Until

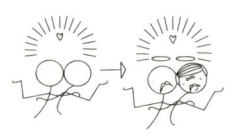

I will be your best friend until the end

It is still very cold in my room today 오늘도 내 방은 여전히 매우 춥다 **Do we really have to break up, my love?** 우리 정말로 헤어지야만 하겠어 내 사랑? **I will be your best friend until the end** 나는 마지막까지 너의 가장 친한 친구일 것이다

I wish to go to the ball with him 나는 그와 무도회에 가고 싶다 **Have you tried to back up a friend before?** 전에 친구를 도우려고 시도했던 적이 있나? **I must find my money first before I leave** 나는 떠나기 전에 먼저 나의 돈을 찾아야 한다

121

Part

Your part in the play is really very important

122

Draw

Can you draw a big house on this paper?

123

Right

Can you tell me if this sentence is right?

Your part in the play is really very important 그 연극에서 너의 역할은 아주 중요하다
Can you draw a big house on this paper? 너는 이 종이에 커다란 집을 그릴 수 있겠니?
Can you tell me if this sentence is right? 너는 이 문장이 올바른지 내게 말해줄 수 있겠니?

124

Of

I do not think we have enough of that

125

Big

Do you want to live in a big house?

126

Writes

I think she writes for the high school paper

I do not think we have enough of that 나는 우리가 그것을 충분히 가졌다고 생각하지 않는다
Do you want to live in a big house? 너는 큰 집에 살고 싶니? I think she writes for the high school paper 나는 그녀가 고등학교 신문에 기고한다고 생각한다

We wanted to see the making of that show 우리는 그 쇼의 제작 과정을 보고 싶어했다
The children knew they have to grow up fast 아이들은 그들이 빨리 자라야 한다는 것을 알았다
She told me about the break up with you 그녀가 내게 너와의 이별에 대해 말했다

130 Was — I heard she was not that good in class

131 Play — I really wanted to go with them and play

132 Idea — I have a great idea for my new house

I heard she was not that good in class 나는 그녀가 수업에서 그리 잘하지 못했다고 들었다   I really wanted to go with them and play 나는 정말로 그들과 함께 가서 놀고 싶었다   I have a great idea for my new house 나에게 새 집에 대한 멋진 생각이 있다

133 Talked — He just talked and talked for a long time

134 My — I just saw a great example before my eyes

135 Waited — The class waited for an hour in the room

He just talked and talked for a long time 그는 오랫동안 말하고 또 말했다 I just saw a great example before my eyes 나는 방금 내 눈 앞에서 훌륭한 예를 보았다 The class waited for an hour in the room 그 학급은 그 방에서 한 시간 동안 기다렸다

136

Much

Once in your life you will love so much

137

Walks

She walks with me in the park every morning

138

With

I want to eat out with my mother today

Once in your life you will love so much 너의 인생에서 한 번은 매우 사랑하게 될 것이다 She walks with me in the park every morning 그녀는 매일 아침 나와 공원에서 산책한다 I want to eat out with my mother today 나는 오늘 어머니와 외식하기를 원한다

139
Sun

Many people asked about the story of the sun

140
Through

Most people do not know what she went through

141
Wish

I wish that she heard what I told her

Many people asked about the story of the sun 많은 사람들이 그 태양의 이야기에 대해 물었다 **Most people do not know what she went through** 대부분의 사람들은 그녀가 무슨 일을 겪었는지 모른다 **I wish that she heard what I told her** 나는 내가 그녀에게 한 말을 그녀가 들었기를 바란다

142

Can

How can I not like a man like Youngchoon?

143

Wait

I did not wait this long just for nothing!

144

Youngchoon

Youngchoon and his family will live in that house

How can I not like a man like Youngchoon? 어떻게 내가 영춘 같은 남자를 좋아하지 않을 수 있겠어? **I did not wait this long just for nothing!** 나는 아무 이유 없이 이렇게 오래 기다리지 않았어! **Youngchoon and his family will live in that house** 영춘과 그의 가족은 그 집에서 살 것이다

145
How

Do you know how much you mean to me?

146
As

I want to run as fast as I can

147
Still

Will you still love him after what he did?

Do you know how much you mean to me? 너는 나에게 얼마나 큰 의미인지 알고 있나?
I want to run as fast as I can 나는 할 수 있는 한 빠르게 달리기를 원한다 **Will you still love him after what he did?** 그가 그런 짓을 한 뒤에도 여전히 그를 사랑할 거니?

The children want to play with the new teacher 그 아이들은 새로운 선생님과 놀고 싶어한다 There were several men behind the big old house 크고 오래된 집 뒤에 몇몇 남자들이 있었다 My students will run to the park with me 나의 학생들과 함께 공원까지 달릴 것이다

151
Died
I heard him call your name before he died

152
Say
You have to say what is inside of you

153
Hot
The new teacher in Korea high is so hot!

I heard him call your name before he died 나는 그가 죽기 전에 너의 이름을 부르는 것을 들었다 **You have to say what is inside of you** 너는 당신의 안에 무엇이 있는지 이야기해야 한다 **The new teacher in Korea high is so hot!** 한국 고등학교의 새로운 교사는 너무 섹시하다!

154

Other

I hope we could talk with each other today

155

Known

I have known him since I was a child

156

Does

He does not want to talk to my mother

I hope we could talk with each other today 나는 오늘 우리가 서로 이야기할 수 있기를 바란다   **I have known him since I was a child** 나는 어릴 때부터 그를 알아왔다
He does not want to talk to my mother 그는 나의 어머니와 이야기하기를 원하지 않았다

157

Part

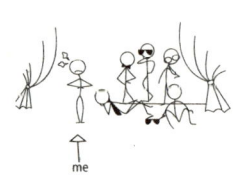

I do not like my part in the play

158

Talk

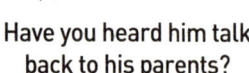

Have you heard him talk back to his parents?

159

He

I waited for him but he did not come

I do not like my part in the play 나는 그 연극에서 역할이 마음에 들지 않는다　**Have you heard him talk back to his parents?** 그가 부모님께 말대답 하는 걸 들었니?　**I waited for him but he did not come** 나는 그를 기다렸지만 오지 않았다

160

In

He left a letter for her in the car

161

Live

I am not ready to live in the city

162

The

I saw the little man smiling at my teacher

He left a letter for her in the car 그는 자동차 안에 그녀를 위한 편지를 남겼다   I am not ready to live in the city 나는 도시에서 살 준비가 되어있지 않다   I saw the little man smiling at my teacher 나는 그 작은 남자가 나의 선생님에게 미소 짓는 것을 보았다

I play three different parts in the school play 나는 학교 연극에서 세 가지 다른 역할을 한다 **I want to play with my three children later** 나는 나중에 세 명의 아이들과 놀기를 원한다 **There is a school in front of my house** 나의 집 앞에 학교가 있다

166 Those — I want to grow old with those intelligent people

167 Time — His friend has known him for a long time

168 Table — I saw the letter on the table this morning

I want to grow old with those intelligent people 나는 그 지적인 사람들과 함께 늙어가고 싶다 His friend has known him for a long time 그의 친구들은 그를 오랫동안 알아왔다 I saw the letter on the table this morning 나는 오늘 아침 탁자 위에 있는 편지를 보았다

169

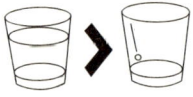

Much

How much money do you make in a day?

170

Living

How much money do you make for a living?

171

City

Do you know how to go to the city?

How much money do you make in a day? 너는 하루에 얼마나 많은 돈을 버니?
How much money do you make for a living? 너는 생계를 위해 얼마나 많은 돈을 버니?
Do you know how to go to the city? 너는 그 도시에 어떻게 가는지 아니?

172
Half

Half of the class asked for a new teacher

173
Morning

They will move to the country in the morning

174
Hope

A great love is the hope of every man

Half of the class asked for a new teacher 학급의 절반이 새로운 교사를 요구했다
They will move to the country in the morning 그들은 아침에 시골로 갈 것이다
A great love is the hope of every man 위대한 사랑은 모든 남자의 꿈이다

175
Got

I want to know where you got that story

176
Some

Some of them left their house in the morning

177
Attending

Some of my students will be attending the ball

I want to know where you got that story 네가 어디서 그 이야기를 들었는지 알고 싶다
Some of them left their house in the morning 그들 중 몇몇은 아침에 집을 떠났다 **Some of my students will be attending the ball** 나의 학생들 중 몇몇이 무도회에 참석할 것이다

Did you hear the important thing she had said? 그녀가 말했던 중요한 것을 들었니?
A man went through the door without a sound 한 남자가 소리 없이 문으로 들어왔다
Did you hear what she just told the teacher? 그녀가 방금 선생님에게 뭐라고 말했는지 들었니?

181

Inside

The old ball was found inside the blue car

182

Boy

The little boy next to him started to run

183

Who

She knew the man who asked her for money

The old ball was found inside the blue car 그 낡은 공이 그 파란색 치 인에서 발견되었다   The little boy next to him started to run 그의 옆에 있던 어린 소년이 달리기 시작했다   She knew the man who asked her for money 그녀는 그녀에게 돈을 요구했던 남자를 알았다

184

Big

The first family will live in that big house

185

Best

My best friend will go to Korea with me

186

Story

My mother told me a very funny love story

The first family will live in that big house 첫 번째 가족이 저 큰 집에서 살 것이다
My best friend will go to Korea with me 나의 가장 친한 친구는 나와 함께 한국에 갈 것이다 **My mother told me a very funny love story** 나의 어머니는 아주 재미있는 사랑 이야기를 들려주었다

187
Ride

My friend will give me a ride home later

188
Thought

She thought she could help him find his house

189
Young

Some students in our school are still very young

My friend will give me a ride home later 나의 친구가 나중에 나를 집까지 태워다 줄 것이다 **She thought she could help him find his house** 그녀는 자신이 그가 그의 집을 찾는 일을 도울 수 있다고 생각했다 **Some students in our school are still very young** 우리 학교의 몇몇 학생들은 여전히 아주 어리다

190

Went

My teacher went to our house with my friend

191

High

She will go to a high school in Korea

192

New

My father gave my mother a big new house

My teacher went to our house with my friend 나의 선생님이 내 친구와 함께 우리 집으로 갔다   She will go to a high school in Korea 그녀는 한국에 있는 고등학교에 갈 것이다   My father gave my mother a big new house 나의 아버지는 어머니에게 커다란 새 집을 선물했다

9words

193

Those

Those students must run to school to be early

194

Car

The car must move to the left right now

195

Best

My room is the best one in our house

Those students must run to school to be early 그 학생들은 학교에 일찍 가려면 뛰어야 한다 **The car must move to the left right now** 그 차는 지금 당장 왼쪽으로 움직여야 한다 **My room is the best one in our house** 나의 방은 우리 집에서 가장 좋은 방이다

196

Soon

I know why he will leave the room soon

197

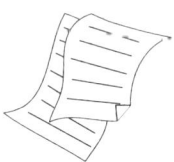

Paper

My teacher said she could not find my paper

198

Youngchoon

I have to hand in my paper to Youngchoon

I know why he will leave the room soon 나는 그가 그 방을 아주 빨리 떠났는지 안다
My teacher said she could not find my paper 나의 선생님은 그녀가 나의 시험지를 찾을 수 없었다고 말했다 I have to hand in my paper to Youngchoon 나는 서류를 영춘에게 제출해야 한다

199

Known

My best friend is a known teacher in Korea

200

Men

The men saw the students jogging in the park

201

Students

The students saw the children dancing in the park

My best friend is a known teacher in Korea 나의 가장 친한 친구는 한국에서 유명한 교사다 **The men saw the students jogging in the park** 그 남자들은 공원에서 조깅하는 학생들을 보았다 **The students saw the children dancing in the park** 그 학생들은 공원에서 춤추는 아이들을 보았다

My parents will be back from their break today 나의 부모님이 오늘 그들의 휴가에서 돌아오실 것이다 **The students will be back from their break today** 그 학생들은 오늘 휴가에서 돌아올 것이다 **I know nothing about the story of the teacher** 나는 그 선생님의 이야기에 대해 아무 것도 모른다

205

Blue

The brown room is better than the blue room

206

Before

You have to eat before you leave the house

207

On

Just keep on jogging until you find his house

The brown room is better than the blue room 그 갈색 방은 파란색 방보나 낫다
You have to eat before you leave the house 너는 집을 나서기 전에 먹어야 한다 Just keep on jogging until you find his house 그냥 그의 집을 찾을 때까지 조깅을 계속해라

… 9 Words

Review

영춘선생이 일러주는 Review 활용법!

1. 그림과 문장을 보고 의미를 파악합니다
되도록이면 해석을 보지 않고 영어 그대로의
의미를 파악하도록 노력하세요!

2. MP3로 Review 부분을 들으면서 네이티브들의 정확한 발음을 청취합니다
네이티브들의 문장은 두 번씩 반복 됩니다.
처음에는 발음을 청취를 하고 두 번째는 조용히 따라 읽습니다.

3. 이제 Review 부분을 큰 소리 내어 읽습니다
영어는 마음속에 담아두기 위해 배우는 언어가 아닙니다.
마음껏 소리치면서 읽으세요!
단, 전철이나 버스 같은 대중교통에서 책을 읽으시는 분들은
주위 사람들에게 피해가 가지 않게 특별히 조심해 주세요!

★주로 대중교통을 이용하는 영춘선생이 이 책을 들고 다니시는 분을 뵙게 되면
친필 싸인을 즉시 제공하겠습니다.

Review

→ 002

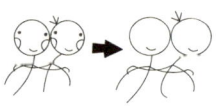

I have known him since I was a child

067 ←

How do you show your love to your parents?

→ 007

We went to the same school in the city

081 ←

I have never known a great man like you

→ 009

He left when both his mother and father died

091 ←

I waited for them but they did not come

→ 199 | 185 ←

My best friend is a known teacher in Korea. | My best friend will go to Korea with me

→ 195 | 168 ←

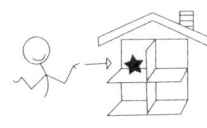 

My room is the best one in our house | I saw the letter on the table this morning

→ 189 | 186 ←

Some students in our school are still very young | My mother told me a very funny love story

→ 014

They started attending a dancing school for young people

097 ←

I have nothing if I do not have you

→ 025

Her best friend was my teacher in high school

098 ←

It is very important that you call her today

→ 031

That boy can run as fast as a car.

105 ←

My parents often give money to the old man

→ 187

My friend will give me a ride home later

144 ←

Youngchoon and his family will live in that house

→ 170

How much money do you make for a living?

138 ←

I want to eat out with my mother today

→ 175

I want to know where you got that story

137 ←

She walks with me in the park every morning

9words **289**

I want to go to your house after school

My teacher asked me to read the short story

My friend and I had a great time last night

I will be your best friend until the end

I did not have enough money to go out

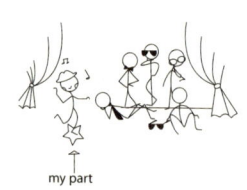

Your part in the play is really very important

How much money do you make in a day?

I really wanted to go with them and play

Some of my students will be attending the ball

My teacher asked me to read the first sentence

The students saw the children dancing in the park

Give me your number so I can call you

→ 122

Can you draw a big house on this paper?

140 ←

Most people do not know what she went through

→ 133

He just talked and talked for a long time

146 ←

I want to run as fast as I can

→ 135

The class waited for an hour in the room

147 ←

Will you still love him after what he did?

The students will be back from their break today

He must have gone out with his best friend

The people in that city died because of fire

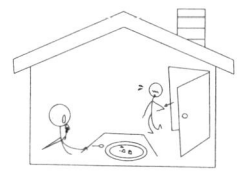

There was no more food when I got home

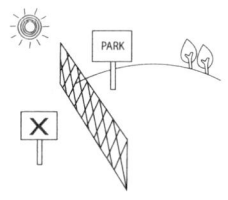

They have to close the park for one day

I could not remember the rest of the show

→ 151

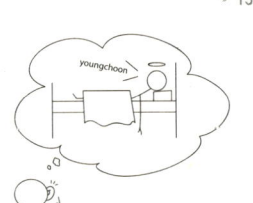

I heard him call your name before he died

163 ←

I play three different parts in the school play

→ 152

You have to say what is inside of you

159 ←

I waited for him but he did not come

→ 157

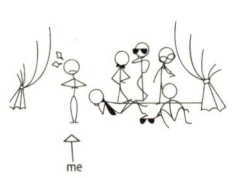

I do not like my part in the play

165 ←

There is a school in front of my house

→ 070

I wanted to talk to you about the children

084 ←

He was in the car when I called him

→ 071

Why do you have to leave her so soon?

077 ←

My father has a small house in the country

→ 072

I wanted to talk to you about the play

076 ←

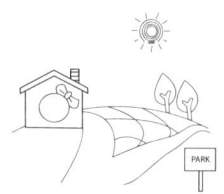

I live in a small house near the park